D1591488

Cultural And
Geographical
Exploration

Robert E. Peary
and the Rush
to the North Pole

CHRONICLES FROM *NATIONAL GEOGRAPHIC*

Cultural And Geographical Exploration

Ancient Civilizations of the Aztecs and Maya

The Ancient Incas

Australia: The Unique Continent

Building the Panama Canal

China's Treasures: The Great Moments

The Hawaiian Islands

Indian Tribes of the American West

Jerusalem and the Holy Land

Lighthouses of the World

Mysteries of the Sahara

Race for the South Pole—The Antarctic Challenge

Rediscovering Ancient Egypt

Robert E. Peary and the Rush to the North Pole

The Russian People in 1914

Surveying the Grand Canyon

Touring America Seventy-Five Years Ago

Cultural And Geographical Exploration

Robert E. Peary and the Rush to the North Pole

CHRONICLES FROM *NATIONAL GEOGRAPHIC*

Arthur M. Schlesinger, jr.
Senior Consulting Editor

Fred L. Israel
General Editor

CHELSEA HOUSE PUBLISHERS

Philadelphia

CHELSEA HOUSE PUBLISHERS

Editor in Chief Stephen Reginald
Managing Editor James D. Gallagher
Production Manager Pamela Loos
Art Director Sara Davis
Director of Photography Judy L. Hasday
Senior Production Editor Lisa Chippendale

First Printing

1 3 5 7 9 8 6 4 2

Library of Congress Cataloging-in-Publication Data

Robert E. Peary and the rush to the North Pole: chronicles from National Geographic/
Arthur M. Schlesinger, senior consulting editor, Fred L. Israel, general editor.
p.   cm.—(Cultural and geographical exploration)
Includes bibliographical references and index.
Summary: Articles originally published in "National Geographic" present the life
and accomplishments of Robert E. Peary, focusing on his explorations of the
North Pole.
ISBN 0-7910-5099-8
1. Peary, Robert E. (Robert Edwin), 1856–1920—Juvenile literature.
2. North Pole—Discovery and exploration—Juvenile literature.
3. Explorers—United States—Biography—Juvenile literature.
[1. Peary, Robert E. (Robert Edwin), 1856–1920.
2. Explorers. 3. North Pole—Discovery and exploration.]
I. Schlesinger, Arthur Meier, 1917–   .   II. Israel, Fred L.   III. Series.
G635.P4R59   1999
919.804ı092—dc21   98-32303
[B]   CIP
                                                                    AC

CONTENTS

"THE GREATEST EDUCATIONAL JOURNAL"

When the first *National Geographic* magazine appeared in October 1888, the United States totaled 38 states. Grover Cleveland was President. The nation's population hovered around 60 million. Great Britain's Queen Victoria also ruled as the Empress of India. William II became Kaiser of Germany that year. Tsar Alexander III ruled Russia and the Turkish Empire stretched from the Balkans to the tip of Arabia. To Westerners, the Far East was still a remote and mysterious land. Throughout the world, riding the back of an animal was the principle means of transportation. Unexplored and unmarked places dotted the global map.

On January 13, 1888, thirty-three men—scientists, cartographers, inventors, scholars, and explorers—met in Washington, D. C. They had accepted an invitation from Gardiner Greene Hubbard (1822-1897), the first president of the Bell Telephone Co. and a leader in the education of the deaf, to form the National Geographic Society "to increase and diffuse geographic knowledge." One of the assembled group noted that they were the "first explorers of the Grand Canyon and the Yellowstone, those who had carried the American flag farthest north, who had measured the altitude of our famous mountains, traced the windings of our coasts and rivers, determined the distribution of flora and fauna, enlightened us in the customs of the aborigines, and marked out the path of storm and flood." Nine months later, the first issue of *National Geographic* magazine was sent out to 165 charter members. Today, more than a century later, membership has grown to an astounding 11 million in more than 170 nations. Several times that number regularly read the monthly issues of the *National Geographic* magazine.

The first years were difficult ones for the new magazine. The earliest volumes seem dreadfully scientific and quite dull. The articles in Volume I, No. 1 set the tone—W. M Davis, "Geographic Methods in Geologic Investigation," followed by W. J. McGee, "The Classification of Geographic Forms by Genesis." Issues came out erratically—three in 1889, five in 1890, four in 1891; and two in 1895. In January 1896 "an illustrated monthly" was added to the title. The November issue that year contained a photograph of a half-naked Zulu bride and bridegroom in their wedding finery staring full face into the camera. But, a reader must have wondered what to make of the accompanying text: "These people . . . possess some excellent traits, but are horribly cruel when once they have smelled blood." In hopes of expanding circulation, the Board of Managers offered newsstand copies at $.25 each and began to accept advertising. But the magazine essentially remained unchanged. Circulation only rose slightly.

In January 1898, shortly after Gardiner Greene Hubbard's death, his son-in-law Alexander Graham Bell (1847-1922) agreed to succeed him as the second president of the National Geographic Society. Bell invented the telephone in 1876 and, while pursuing his life long goal of improving the lot of the deaf, had turned his amazingly versatile mind to contemplating such varied problems as human flight, air conditioning, and popularizing geography. The society then had about 1100 members—the magazine was on the edge of bankruptcy. Bell did not want the job. He wrote in his diary though that he accepted leadership of the Society "in order to save it. Geography is a fascinating subject and it can be made interesting," he told the board of directors. Bell abandoned the unsuccessful attempt to increase circulation through newsstand sales. "Our journal," he wrote "should go to members, people who believe in our work and want to help." He understood that the lure for prospective members should be an association with a society that made it possible for the average person to share with kings and scientists the excitement of sending an expedition to a strange land or an explorer to an inaccessible region. This idea, more than any other, has been responsible for the growth of the National Geographic Society and for the popularity of the magazine. "I can well remember," recalled Bell in 1912, "how the idea was laughed at that we should ever reach a membership of ten thousand." That year it had soared to 107,000!

Bell attributed this phenomenal growth though to one man who had transformed the *National Geographic* magazine into "the greatest educational journal in the world"—Gilbert H. Grosvenor (1875-1966). Bell had hired the then 24-year-old Grosvenor in 1899 as the Society's first full-time employee "to put some life into the magazine." He personally escorted the new editor, who will become his son-in-law, to the Society's headquarters—a small rented room shared with the American Forestry Association on the fifth floor of a building, long since gone, across 15th street from the U. S. Treasury in downtown Washington. Grosvenor remembered the headquarters "littered with old magazines, newspapers, and a few record books and six enormous boxes crammed with *Geographics* returned by the newsstands." "No desk!" exclaimed Bell. "I'll send you mine." That afternoon, delivery men brought Grosvenor a large walnut rolltop and the new editor began to implement Bell's instructions—to transform the magazine from one of cold geographic fact "expressed in hieroglyphic terms which the layman could not understand into a vehicle for carrying the living, breathing, human-interest truth about this great world of ours to the people." And what did Bell consider appropriate "geographic subjects?" He replied: "The world and all that is in it is our theme."

Grosvenor shared Bell's vision of a great society and magazine which would disseminate geographic knowledge. "I thought of geography in terms of its Greek root: *geographia*—a description of the world," he later wrote. "It thus becomes the most catholic of subjects, universal in appeal, and embracing nations, people, plants, birds, fish. We would never lack interesting subjects." To attract readers, Grosvenor had to change the public attitude toward geography which he knew was regarded as "one of the dullest of all subjects, something to inflict upon schoolboys and avoid in later life." He wondered why certain books which relied heavily on geographic description remained popular—Charles Darwin's *Voyage of the Beagle*, Richard Dana, Jr.'s *Two Years Before the Mast* and even Herodotus' *History*. Why did readers for generations, and with Herodotus' travels, for twenty centuries return to these books? What did these volumes, which used so many geographic descriptions, have in common? What was the secret? According to Grosvenor, the answer was that "each was an accurate, eyewitness, firsthand account. Each contained simple straightforward writing—writing that sought to make pictures in the reader's mind."

Gilbert Grosvenor was editor of the *National Geographic* magazine for 55 years, from 1899 until 1954. Each of the 660 issues under his direction had been a highly readable geography textbook. He took Bell's vision and made it a reality. Acclaimed as "Mr. Geography," he discovered the earth anew for himself and for millions around the globe. He charted the dynamic course which the National Geographic Society and its magazine followed for more than half a century. In so doing, he forged an instrument for world education and understanding unique in this or any age. Under his direction, the *National Geographic* magazine grew from a few hundred copies—he recalled carrying them to the post office on his back—to more than five million at the time of his retirement as editor, enough for a stack 25 miles high.

This Chelsea House series celebrates Grosvenor's first twenty-five years as editor of the *National Geographic*. "The mind must see before it can believe," said Grosvenor. From the earliest days, he filled the magazine with photographs and established another Geographic principle—to portray people in their natural attire or lack of it. Within his own editorial committee, young Grosvenor encountered the prejudice that photographs had to be "scientific." Too often, this meant dullness. To Grosvenor, every picture and sentence had to be interesting to the layman. "How could you educate and inform if you lost your audience by boring your readers?" Grosvenor would ask his staff. He persisted and succeeded in making the *National Geographic* magazine reflect this fascinating world.

To the young-in-heart of every age there is magic in the name *National Geographic*. The very words conjure up enchanting images of faraway places, explorers and scientists, sparkling seas and dazzling mountain peaks, strange plants, animals, people, and customs. The small society founded in 1888 "for the increase and diffusion of geographic knowledge" grew, under the guidance of one man, to become a great force for knowledge and understanding. This achievement lies in the genius of Gilbert H. Grosvenor, the architect and master builder of the National Geographic Society and its magazine.

Fred L. Israel
The City College of the City University of New York

ROBERT E. PEARY

FRED L. ISRAEL

The geographic North Pole marks the northernmost point on earth. American explorer Robert E. Peary (1856-1920) led the first expedition usually credited with reaching the Pole. The expedition included Matthew Henson, an African-American who had accompanied Peary on his explorations for over twenty years. They made the trip by dog sled in 1909.

Peary was a great Arctic explorer. His 1886 experience in mapping the interior of Greenland convinced him to undertake further expeditions.

In 1891, Peary confirmed that Greenland is an island. He brought back detailed information about the area as well as ethnological studies of little known Eskimo tribes. Other trips between 1893 and 1897 resulted in important scientific discoveries about the arctic region. Peary wrote of these adventures in *Northward Over the Great Ice* (1898).

In 1898, Peary set out to reach the North Pole. He had concluded that the practical route for reaching it was for his ship to go as far north as possible to a winter harbor on the Greenland coast—and then by dog sled due north. In January 1899, after a sled journey over difficult ice with temperatures considerably below zero, Peary's feet froze necessitating the amputation of eight toes. However, in a few weeks, he was in the field again with his seemingly boundless energy. This expedition reached a latitude about 390 miles south of the Pole before severe weather conditions forced him back. He returned to the United States in 1902 after four years in the Arctic.

In 1905, Peary again tried to reach the North Pole. He now was encouraged by President Theodore Roosevelt, who had followed enthusiastically Peary's polar exploits. "The attainment of the Pole should be your main object. Nothing short will suffice," wrote Roosevelt who agreed with Peary that the glory of reaching the North Pole should fall to an American. On April 21, 1906, Peary neared a latitude only 174 miles from his goal, the closest approach up to that time. Unbearable weather, the condition of his dogs, and a declining food supply prevented further progress. It was only after a hazardous trip that the party managed to reach their ship. In December 1906, Peary returned to New York. He published the narrative of this journey in *Nearest the Pole* (1907).

"The lure of the North!" Peary once exclaimed. "It is a strange and powerful thing. More than once I have come back from the great frozen spaces, battered and worn and baffled, sometimes maimed . . . But somehow, it was never many months before the old restless feeling came over me . . . I began to long for the great white desolation, the battles with the ice and the gales, the long, long, long Arctic night, the long, long, long Arctic day, the handful of odd but faithful Eskimos who had been my friends for years, the silence and the vastness of the great, white lovely North. In July 1908, Peary left on his final polar expedition. He was now fifty-two years old. His skill and endurance had been thoroughly tested by a quarter century of Arctic experience. By September, his ship had reached a northern latitude which was a record for any vessel under its own power. The dark winter months were used for making scientific observations and for sleding supplies to Cape Columbia, ninety miles to the northwest from which point he would begin his final assault.

On March 1, 1909, a party of twenty-four men, which included seventeen Eskimos, 133 dogs and nineteen sleds set out from Cape Columbia over the Arctic ice for the Pole. By the end of March, the previous record of "farthest North" was broken. From this point, Peary and Henson, four Eskimos and forty dogs set out for the final dash. On the morning of April 6, Peary's observations showed him to be only three miles from the Pole. He was so exhausted, he thought he could go no further. However, after a few hours sleep, he covered the remaining miles reaching latitude 90 N, and the North Pole. "The Pole at last!!!" he wrote in his diary. "The prize of three centuries, my dream and ambition for twenty-three years. Mine at last."

Peary concluded that the North Pole was definitely located in the center of a vast sea of ice contrary to existing scientific opinion. After 30 hours, during which extensive astronomical observations were made, the party began the return trip. The distance from the Pole to the base camp at Cape Columbia was covered in sixteen days. Peary was ecstatic. He had achieved his goal. Or had he?

On September 5, 1909, Peary's ship reached Indian Harbor, Labrador. From here, he cabled the news that he had reached the North Pole. However, this news came five days after the world had been electrified by the dramatic announcement that Dr. Frederick A. Cook, another polar explorer, who had served as surgeon and ethnologist on Peary's 1891-92 Greenland expedition on April 21, 1908, or a year earlier than Peary. In the bitter public controversy which ensued between the two men and their supporters, the American public was inclined to side with Cook. His sudden appearance after an unheralded expedition, undertaken practically singlehanded, seemed plausible. Cook drew large audiences on his lecture tours and told a convincing story. By contrast, Peary seemed crotchety and bitter.

In October 1909, a committee of experts appointed by the National Geographic Society examined Peary's records and concluded unanimously that Peary had reached the North Pole. In 1911, Congress, after an investigation of the conflicting claims, passed a resolution giving Peary credit for the discovery. The leading American geographic societies also bestowed upon him their highest awards. In large part, these honors recognized Peary's attainment of the North Pole but also were a testament to the value of his Arctic work as a whole. Peary wrote his account of his final Arctic expedition in *The North Pole* (1910).

There is a sequel. In September 1989, almost eight decades after the event, a study sponsored by the National Geographic Society concluded that Peary's navigational measurements had been faulty and he may have been thirty to sixty miles from his goal. "As to whether or not Peary reached the North Pole, the answer," noted the final report, "can never be anything more than a probability." Regardless, Robert E. Peary stands out as a pioneer explorer who conquered man's fear of unknown places.

THE MISSION OF THE "DIANA"

The Peary Arctic Club, under whose patronage Civil Engineer Peary, U. S. N., is now engaged in an expedition to the North Pole, will dispatch the steamship *Diana* about the middle of July on the second of a series of annual reinforcements proposed by Mr. Peary in his original plan of action. The *Diana*, a 427-ton steam barkentine-rigged sealer, built in Greenock in 1871, and thoroughly rebuilt, re-engined, and reclassed in Dundee in 1891, was engaged by the Canadian government during 1897 in the exploration of the water route for commercial purposes between Hudson bay and Liverpool. She is a fast, stanch, and commodious vessel, and the best which has yet been employed in the northern work.

The *Diana* is to be commanded by Capt. Samuel W. Bartlett, of Brigus, Newfoundland, and will be manned by a select crew of Newfoundlanders, familiar with the conditions prevailing in high latitudes. Captain Bartlett is a brother of Capt. John Bartlett, of the *Windward*, and of the late Capt. Harry Bartlett, of the *Falcon*, who were engaged in Peary expeditions. The former has not returned from the expedition of last summer, and the latter was lost with his ship and all on board while returning from Philadelphia to St Johns in the fall of 1894. The *Diana* will carry a scientific party headed by Prof. William Libbey, of Princeton University, for biological and oceanographic work, and a hunting party of four, led by Mr. Russell W. Porter, of Boston. Robert Stein, of the U. S. Geological Survey, of Washington, with two companions, will also sail on the *Diana*, to be landed, if practicable, on Ellesmere land, where he expects to remain for one or two years. Prof. William Libbey, with a complete deep-sea dredging equipment, intends to work at the southern entrance of Smith sound, determining the course and direction of the southward currents, while the Porter party will be taken to the deer and walrus habitats on the Greenland side of the straits.

The *Diana* will take one year's supplies for the *Windward* party, which has not returned, and for her own party, so that in case of any unforeseen accident there will be no danger of lack of food. She will also carry mail and small packages from Norway for Sverdrup, in the *Fram*, who has not been heard from since his departure from Upernavik, July 30, 1898. The itinerary of the *Diana* is that planned by Mr. Peary before leaving for the north last summer. The hope of meeting Peary or his representatives and of obtaining information concerning the winter experiences of the *Windward* and *Fram* parties will make the voyage of this summer one of more than popular scientific interest.

PEARY'S WORK AND PROSPECTS

Peary's latest year in the Arctic, after all allowance has been made, stands as a record of magnificent achievement, and a foundation upon which still greater results are to be attained. The entire country north and west of Cape Sabine, reaching beyond Greely fiord and the eightieth parallel, has been definitely outlined and the confused and utterly inaccurate coastline, sinuous and perplexing to the last degree, of the western side of Smith sound, between Capes Sabine and D'Urville, has been definitely measured and charted. The striking change in the character of the western slope of Grinnell Land is in itself enough to justify and reward the expedition, and will stimulate workers in that most inviting and heretofore neglected field. The hand-to-hand battle against the opposing forces of darkness, frost, and distance which Peary waged during the entire winter makes a chapter daring and effective as any recorded in Arctic history. Where other explorers have waited in more or less impatience, sometimes in comfort and many times in suffering, Peary has been continuously in the field, daunted by no obstacle, and breaking the route along an almost impassable ice-foot for 250 miles. This, too, was not as a mere exploit, but as a practical step in the greater work to be determined next spring. Peary rounded up his year's work with a further personal reconnaissance to the westward, and practically completes twelve months of active work in the open field.

The American people, learning as they will shortly from Peary's own pen the story of the year, cannot fail to feel a sense of pride in their countryman and an excitement of hope that ultimate success may crown his effort to attain the goal of the ages and place his country's flag at the very farthest north. Those who read between the lines and who follow matters practically, find in Peary the mental as well as physical traits, making a combination as rare as the work he has undertaken, coupled with a clear head, and a practical, definite correlation of means to ends, which go far to secure the results desired. Peary will take the field next year, barring unforeseen accidents, a thoroughly sound, rested, and well man, in the very prime of condition, and can be counted on to make a record, even if he does not fully attain his desire. If beaten in 1900, he will try it again in

1901, and maybe again a year later. The very latest word is the very gratifying one that the old *Windward*, battered and scarred from her winter in the ice and stormy passage home, is still sound and seaworthy; that the ship will be repaired, rebuilt, and refitted, and, under an American flag and American master, will return to her contest with the forces of the north, from which she will not come back unless victorious.

H. L. BRIDGMAN.

Brooklyn, N.Y.

PEARY'S EXPLORATIONS IN 1898–1899

"The Mission of the Diana," outlined in THE NATIONAL GEOGRAPHIC MAGAZINE for July (see p. 1), has been successfully carried out in every detail under the able management of Mr. H. L. Bridgman, Secretary of the Peary Arctic Club. More than a year's supplies have been added to the reserve stores of Peary and full accounts obtained of his important explorations during the past twelve months. Thus far merely an outline of his discoveries has been published, but, as Mr. Bridgman has stated in the preceding article, a more detailed account will soon follow.

Instead of reaching Sherard Osborn fiord, on the north coast of Greenland, beyond the narrow channel which all sailing craft must take to reach that part of the globe, Peary was obliged to winter in Kane basin, about 50 miles north of Cape Sabine. His ship stayed in latitude 79°, and not 82°, as he had hoped might be possible. Not having been able to establish his base of sledging operations near Sherard Osborn fiord, he nevertheless ventured northward during the winter four times to Fort Conger, the headquarters of the Greely expedition, a point equally near the Pole, but on the west side of the channel. These long trips were made both for exploration and also to establish caches of supplies along the west side of the channel lead-ing to the north, so that they may be available next spring and during the time the party is engaged in its explorations next summer. These supplies and others that will be added to them will enable Peary to begin his researches on the north coast of Greenland whether or not the *Windward* is able to land her stores at the proposed base in Sherard Osborn fiord.

In the south Peary discovered that the so-called Hayes sound, northwest of Cape Sabine, is only an inlet or bay. It was supposed by many that it extended through to the Arctic ocean west of Ellesmere Land and separated that country from Grinnell Land on the north. Peary's discovery proves that these regions are one and the same land, and he has thus been able to settle one of the most important geographical problems that awaited solution in that region. He also traveled west across the northern part of Ellesmere Land, which has never before been penetrated for any distance, and visited its west coast, joining his survey of the shoreline with the short bit of the coast further north, which Lockwood, of the Greely expedition, discovered in May, 1883. This is the first time that any part of this coast has been seen south of the inlet visited by Lockwood. In his various sledge journeys up the channel from the *Windward*'s position, Peary skirted the east coasts of Grinnell Land and Grant Land for a distance of about 250 miles, rectifying the mapping of this shoreline in some respects, and particularly the surveys of a number of indentations. Fort Conger was the headquarters of the Greely expedition, and Peary was the first to visit the place since Greely left it, in 1883. The most northern point reached by Peary was Cape Beechey, about 82° north latitude. No effort to push northward has been made this summer, and Peary's winter camp has been established on the Greenland side of Smith sound, several miles further south than his quarters of a year ago. Here he has landed all the remaining provisions of the *Windward* and all that the *Diana* brought him.

The *Diana* reports landing the Stein party at Cape Sabine and leaving them in good spirits for a winter in Ellesmere Land. The hunting party led by Russell W. Porter, of Boston, left the ship at various points on the Greenland coast and secured a number of walrus, reindeer, and other game, most of which was added to Peary's stores. Sverdrup in the *Fram* was frozen in near Cocked Hat island, ten miles west of Cape Sabine, where he wintered about 50 miles south of the point reached by Peary. Sverdrup planned this summer to work his ship up Kennedy channel, leaving the *Fram* at some point along the coast for a sledge trip across or around the northern end of Greenland.

PEARY'S WORK IN 1901–1902

FTER four years of brilliant explorations in the far north, Peary has returned to the United States and his last Arctic campaign is ended. A summary of his work during the first three years of this last expedition appeared in the October, 1899, and October, 1901, numbers of this magazine. His work during the past year is summarized in the following modest report to Mr. H. L. Bridgman, secretary of the Peary Arctic Club:

OFFICIAL REPORT BY ROBERT E. PEARY

Dated Sydney, September 7, 1902

Left at Erik Harbor, on the Ellesmere coast, August 29; the party reached Payer Harbor September 16; crossing Rosse Bay partly by sledge and partly by boat, then walked across Bedford Pin Island.

About a week later my Eskimo began to fall sick, not one escaping. By November 19, six adults and one child were dead; nearly all the others very weak, but out of danger. Early in January Eskimo came across from Anoritok,

bringing news of the ravages of a fatal epidemic through the tribe. Word was sent back by these scouts for as many of the survivors as could to come to me, and by the end of the month they began arriving.

In February a large depot of dogfood was established near Cape Louis Napoleon, some 60 miles north of Sabine.

March 3 my advance party of six sledges, in charge of Henson, left for Conger.

March 6 I started with the main party of 18 sledges, leaving Percy in charge at Payer Harbor.

Conger was reached in 12 marches, arriving within an hour or two of the advance party.

My supporting party of Eskimo returning from Conger brought down the instruments, chronometers, and Arctic library.

Eight marches more took us to Cape Hekla. The north end of Robison Channel was all open water to the Greenland coast, and lakes of water extended northward as far as could be seen from Black Cape and Cape Rawson.

From Hekla another supporting party returned.

April 1 I started northward over the polar sea with Henson, four Eskimo, and six sledges.

Old floes covered deep with snow and intersected with rubble ridges and lanes of young ice were encountered from the moment we left the ice foot. The same kind of traveling (except the lanes of young ice) was found by the English expedition of 1876.

After six marches open leads and floes in motion were encountered. Two natives were sent back.

As we advanced the floes became smaller, the pressure ridges on a grander scale, and the open leads more frequent. Each day's march was very tortuous and our general course deflected west by the character of the ice.

Finally at 84° 17′ north latitude, northwest of Hekla, the polar pack became impracticable and further efforts to advance were given up. New leads and pressure ridges, with foggy weather, made our return in some respects more trying than the advance. Hekla was regained April 29 and Conger May 3. Leaving Conger May 6, Cape Sabine on the 17th, a few days later, I went north as far as Cape Louis Napoleon to complete the survey of Dobbin Bay, returning the first of June.

A proposed trip westward across Ellesmereland was prevented by open water in Buchanan Bay. The ice broke up earlier than in 1901, and Payer Harbor was blockaded almost continuously.

The *Windward* bored her way through the ice and entered the harbor on the morning of August 5, and got out the same afternoon, with scarcely 15 minutes to spare before the harbor was closed by the ice. Forcing our way across Smith Sound, my Eskimo with their belongings were landed in Inglefield Gulf, and several days devoted to hunting walrus for their winter subsistence; then the *Windward* started south, reaching and leaving Cape York the afternoon of August 28.

Calling at Godhaven, Greenland, and Cape Haven, Baffinland, the *Windward* arrived at Choteau Bay, Labrador, September 14 and sent dispatches.

The summer voyage has been without mishap, and the *Windward*, with her new engines, has made as good time as the larger and more powerful ships that have been going north the past ten years.

The year at Payer Harbor was passed comfortably, though the anxious strain caused by the ravages of disease among my faithful people was not light. Food was abundant, and our supply of musk ox and deer meat continuous throughout the year.

The northern sledge trip in the spring was arduous, but not marked by special exposure, suffering, or danger more than is necessarily incident to serious Arctic work.

The equipment and personnel was satisfactory, and further advance was vetoed by insuperable natural conditions.

The *Windward* has on board the instruments, chronometers, and Arctic library abandoned by the Greely expedition at Conger, numerous specimens in natural history, bear, musk ox, reindeer, and walrus skins, skeleton of a two-horned narwhal, a rare Arctic specimen; also living specimens of musk ox, walrus, Arctic hare, and Eskimo dogs.

Anchor and chain lost by *Erik* last summer are on board.

The *Fram* left Godhaven about August 20, bound home. She has been in Jones Sound, from whence it is understood explorations were made to the northwest. One death, a fireman, is reported since 1899. Others on board said to be well.

The little schooner *Forgetmenot*, caught in the ice at Cape Haven last year, is now on her way to St Johns.

(Signed)   PEARY.

SUMMARY OF PEARY'S WORK

Mr. Peary has devoted practically the whole of the last twelve years to Arctic work. He announces that he has now retired from Arctic exploration and will hereafter devote his energies to his profession, civil engineering. The results of his long labors in the far north are most important. He has proved Greenland an island and mapped its northern coast line; he has defined and mapped the islands to the north of Greenland, known as the Greenland Archipelago; he has shown that an ice-covered Arctic ocean probably extends from the Greenland Archipelago to the North Pole; he has accurately defined the lands opposite the northwestern coast of Greenland, Grant Land, Grinnell Land, and Ellesmereland; he has reached the most north-erly known land in the world; he has gained the most northerly point yet reached on the Western Hemisphere, 84° 17′; he has studied the Eskimo as only one can who has lived with them for years; he has added much to our knowledge of Arctic fauna and flora; of the musk ox, the Arctic hare, and the deer; the notes he has made during the past years will benefit meteorology and geology—all these are some of Lieutenant Peary's achievements during the twelve years he has so valiantly battled in the far north. But, above all, Mr. Peary has given the world a notable example of a brave and modest man who, in spite of broken limbs and most terrible physical suffering and financial discouragements, has unflinchingly forced to a successful end that which he had decided to accomplish.

To Mrs. Peary, the able seconder of her husband's plans, and to Mr. H. L. Bridgman, the efficient secretary of the Peary Arctic Club, and the loyal members of that club, much credit is due.

G. H. G.

PEARY ON THE NORTH POLE

IN a lecture before the National Geographic Society November 29, 1902, Commander Robert E. Peary stated very emphatically that he believed the North Pole could be reached by making Cape Hekla, in northern Grinnell Land, the starting point for the sledging trip north. The average distance of Peary's four Arctic sledge journeys over the ice is slightly greater than the distance from Hekla to the Pole and back. If the next arctic explorer will make Cape Hekla his base, will pass the winter there, and starting from that point in spring fight his way as many miles northward over the ice as Peary averaged in his four journeys under equal conditions, he will gain the Pole itself and have ample time to return before the ice pack becomes impassable. To quote from Mr. Peary's address:

"There are two facts I wish to bring to your attention, not in a boastful manner, but as bearing upon the feasibility of reaching the Pole. First, the average air-line distance from start to finish of four sledge journeys which I have made in high arctic latitudes is the same as the distance from the northern shore of Grinnell Land to the Pole. Second, the air-line distance from start to finish of my 1900 sledge journey is such that had my starting point been in the same latitude as that of Abruzzi it would have taken me to the Pole, or had my starting point been in the same latitude as Nansen's or on the northern shore of Grinnell Land, it would have carried me beyond the Pole.

"It may seem to indicate overconfidence to state boldly that the Pole can be reached, and yet it is a fact, even though the struggle for it has been going on unsuccessfully for years and years. Each time we have come a little nearer, each time we have learned a little more, and I say to you here tonight that it is not an impossibility; that it can be done, and that it is no more difficult than many of the great projects which we see being pushed to completion every day and which require money, persistence, hard work, and some ability to bring the full fruition.

"The man who can secure a starting point in early spring on the northern coast of Grinnell Land, who has with him the proper party and the proper equipment and experience, will hold within his grasp the last geographical prize that the earth has to offer—the prize which will rank with the prize which Columbus won for himself and his countrymen, a fame which will last as long as human life exists on the globe."

New York, October 17, 1902.

Commander Robert E. Peary, U.S.N.
Washington, D.C.,

Dear Sir:-

The Peary Arctic Club acknowledges your preliminary report of the 17th ult. and letter of the 4th inst., and extends to you its cordial welcome upon your return to country and home. It honors you for patience, courage and fortitude, undaunted by formidable obstacles; thanks you for the wise and effective use of the means placed at your disposal, and congratulates you upon your achievements memorable in the annals of science and discovery.

Assuring you of our appreciation and regard, we subscribe ourselves -

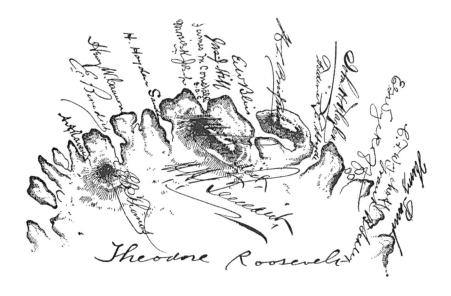

PEARY AND THE NORTH POLE

THE announcement of Commander Robert E. Peary that he is to make one more attempt to reach the North Pole has been received with much enthusiasm. Every one has been hoping that he would be able to carry out the plan which he has adopted for his next Arctic campaign, a plan which he outlined some months ago when it was doubtful whether he would ever go north again. This plan differs in one very important respect from all his former campaigns in that he proposes to make his winter camp fully one hundred miles north of his previous winter quarters; so that when he is ready to start on his dash in spring he will be 100 miles nearer his goal. The distance thus saved—from Cape Sabine to Cape Joseph Henry—is the most difficult of traverse, and to overcome it has in the past taken several weeks of the short working season.

The distance from Peary's proposed winter camp near Cape Joseph Henry to the Pole and back again is less than the average distance of four sledging trips which he has made, and each of these trips was over rougher ice than it is believed will be encountered beyond the 84th parallel. Mr. Peary will start north in July, 1904.

He hopes to be able to reach Cape Joseph Henry with his vessel in the fall of that year, and to make his dash in 1905. In case be does not reach the cape in 1904, he will spend 1905 in getting there, and make his dash in 1906. His plan is outlined in the following letter, addressed to the Secretary of the Navy, asking for three years' leave of absence:

WASHINGTON, D. C.,
September 2, 1903.

SIR: Referring to my application for leave of absence accompanying this, I beg to state for your information that I propose to secure a suitable ship, put her into one of our best shipyards, have her reenforced and strengthened to the maximum degree and fitted with American engines, possessing the maximum of strength and power with the minimum weight and space, so that she may go north as an exponent of American skill and mechanical ability.

With such ship I should sail north about the 1st of next July, and on reaching the Whale Sound region should take on board my Eskimo, establish my permanent sub-base at Cape Sabine, and then force my way northward to my proposed winter quarters on the northern shore of Grant Land, establishing caches as far as practicable en route. By the earliest returning light of the following February I should start due north over the polar pack with a small, light pioneer party, followed by a large, heavy main party. I should expect to accomplish the distance to the Pole and return in about 100 days or a little more, an average travel of about 10 miles a day. Returning, I should break the ship out late in the same season and return home.

If ice conditions the first year were such as to prevent reaching the northern shore of Grant Land, I should winter as far north as practicable and force the ship to the desired location the following year. In this event the expedition would be gone two years.

This plan is the result of some twelve years of almost continuous experience in those latitudes, and is based upon an extended personal acquaintance with the region from Sabine to 84° north latitude and a thorough familiarity with climatic and other conditions and with Eskimo.

The distinctive features of my plan are: The use of individual sledges with comparatively light loads, drawn by dogs, giving a traveling unit of high speed and radius of reach, as opposed to the man sledge, with its heavy load, slow speed, and limited radius; the adoption of Eskimo methods and costume and the fullest utilization of the Eskimo themselves.

The advantage of my plan and route are a fixed land base 100 miles nearer the Pole than on any other route, a more rigid ice pack extending Poleward than is to be found on the opposite side of the Pole, a wider land base upon which to retreat, and a well-beaten line of communication and retreat from winter quarters to comparatively low latitudes, which is practicable at any season of the year.

The work outlined above comprises two distinct stages, viz., the navigation of the ship to the northern shore of Grant Land, the traverse of the polar pack with sledges from the northern shore of Grant Land to the Pole and return. In connection with the former, four ships (the *Polaris*, the *Alert*, the *Discovery*, and the *Proteus*) have accomplished this feat. In regard to the second, I have already made four trips in those same regions, in which the average air-line distance from start to finish was the same as the distance from Grant Land to the Pole. The air-line distance from start to finish of my 1900 sledge journey was such that had my starting point been the north-

ern shore of Grant Land it would have carried me beyond the Pole and return. I beg to state for your consideration the following:

The North Pole is the last great geographical prize the earth has to offer. Its attainment will be accepted as the sign of man's final physical conquest of the globe, and it will always stand as one of the great milestones in the world's history.

The attainment of the North Pole is, in my opinion, our manifest privilege and duty. Its attainment by another country would be in the light of a reproach and criticism.

The sense of all the foremost geographers, practical and theoretical, now converges upon the Smith Sound or "American route," along which I have been working for years past. Other routes have been eliminated. If we delay in preëmpting this route some one else will step in and win the prize.

I believe that my experience, gained in years of practical work; my special methods of travel and equipment, the evolution of years of practical work; my personal acquaintance with every feature of my chosen route and region, and my command of the full resources and utmost efforts of the entire little tribe of Whale Sound hyperboreans, who have lived and worked with me for years, give substantial reasons for anticipating a successful outcome to an expedition based on the above lines.

Very respectfully,
R. E. PEARY,
Civil Engineer, U. S. N.

The reply of Hon. Charles H. Darling, Acting Secretary of the Navy, granting Mr. Peary's application, is as follows:

DEAR SIR: In granting you leave of absence for the purpose of prosecuting your Arctic work, I am moved to remark that I believe you are better equipped than any other person in the country to undertake this work. You have the requisite courage, fortitude, and physique. You have had a longer term of service within the Arctic circle than any other explorer. You have had large experience in sledge journeying, both upon the land and upon the polar pack. You are familiar with ice conditions through the Smith Sound route and north of Grant Land and the continent. You have demonstrated your ability to maintain yourself in that latitude for a longer period in health and safety than any other explorer. You have reduced the inconveniences and hardships of the Arctic service to a minimum.

You are conversant with the language and customs of the Whale Sound Esquimaux and are personally acquainted with every individual in the tribe.

They have become accustomed to your leadership, and if you succeed in transporting the selected hunters and the best families to the north shore of Grant Land, as you propose, you will thereby establish a base which will enable you to live in safety and comparative comfort for an indefinite period.

Grant Land as such base has great advantages over Spitzbergen, Franz Josef Land, or any other known point, in that it has an extensive shore line, which a party retreating from the Pole cannot fail to find, whatever may be the extent of the polar drift.

In establishing a colony of Esquimaux at this point, you thereby establish a self-sustaining base at the nearest practicable point to the Pole. Such self-sustaining base has not heretofore been established in any such high latitude. Your ability to force your ships to a high northing with this Esquimau colony is all important to your success. Such northing has been made by the *Polaris*, the *Alert*, the *Discovery*, and the *Proteus*. There would seem to be no reason why you can not do the same. Knowledge of ice conditions that has been gained since that time will certainly enable you to provide a ship better adapted to the purpose than either one of these.

The attainment of the Pole should be your main object. Nothing short will suffice. The discovery of the Poles is all that remains to complete the map of the world. That map should be completed in our generation and by our countrymen. If it is claimed that the enterprise is fraught with danger and privation, the answer is that geographical discovery in all ages has been purchased at the price of heroic courage and noble sacrifice. Our national pride is involved in the undertaking, and this department expects that you will accomplish your purpose and bring further distinction to a service of illustrious traditions.

In conclusion, I am pleased to inform you that the President of the United States sympathizes with your cause and approves the enterprise.

With best wishes for your health and confidence in your success,

I am, respectfully,

CHARLES H. DARLING,

Acting Secretary.

The Peary Arctic Club, which so generously supported Mr. Peary's explorations 1898–1902, have contributed the funds that make this new expedition possible.

ADDRESS BY COMMANDER ROBERT E. PEARY, U. S. N.

President Eighth International Geographic Congress

On the Assembling of the Congress in Washington September 8, 1904

Gentlemen, Delegates, and Members of the Eighth International Geographic Congress:

FOR the first time, America welcomes you and is honored by your presence. For the first time we have the pride and pleasure of extending a hearty greeting to our distinguished friends and co-workers in the great mother science, gathered from the civilized nations of the world.

For the eighth time since its inception the International Geographic Congress meets to note the progress of discovery, to listen to the results of the researches of its Fellows, and to suggest and plan for the future.

Seven times it has met in the great capitals of Europe; now it meets in the capital of your young but buxom sister of America.

Numbers of you meet here again comrades of previous Congresses. Others have attended their last Congress, and survive only in their works.

Stanley and Nordenskjold, captains of the tropics and the Arctic, have passed away in the quiet of their homes, their strenuous work ended years ago.

Daly and Du Chaillu have died amid the peaceful surroundings of civilization.

Andrée and Toll have met their fate in the stress of struggle with the icy North.

There have been numerous "world happenings" since the last Congress, which, while not purely geographical, it may be well perhaps to note here.

When the last Congress met a struggle had been finished in the distant East far-reaching in its effects; the beginning of a new policy, a new line of thought and action, the first step in the inevitable and inexorable destiny of this country.

At the present time another struggle is going on in the same region, fateful with the greatest possibilities to two of our friends and neighbors.

Since the last Congress two republics have ceased to exist in Africa and a new one has been born in America.

In Asia a great new line of communication has been completed—the Trans-Siberian Railway.

Along the wide floor of the Pacific a world nerve vibrates today which did not exist when you last met—the new Pacific cable.

Wireless telegraphy is an accomplished fact today, not an experiment, and the atmosphere of the globe in a short time will throb incessantly with countless messages.

Finally, there is that vision of the centuries, that envious dream of monarchs and ministers since Gomara quested for the "Secret of the Strait" four hundred years ago—the Isthmian Canal, the union of the Atlantic and the Pacific—the grandest project, the greatest engineering, financial, and diplomatic problem of the age.

A fearless master hand has at a stroke cut the Gordian tangle that has hitherto defied the ablest statesmen and financiers of the world, and the nations today accept without question the Panama Canal as a fact.

A few years hence and the commerce of the world will pass freely from the eastern sea to the western sea, traversing almost air lines from port to port, at an enormous saving of time and distance and expense, and this great orient-and-occident-facing Republic will rest content with

coasts united from Eastport to the Straits of Fuca.

Much has been done in the geographical world since the last Congress, both in the field and in the study, and the number of possible great discoveries is rapidly narrowing every year.

Only two great prizes now wait the present-day explorer—the North Pole and the South Pole.

It is interesting to note how, from Congress to Congress, the scene of geographical interest shifts from one region to another.

Africa, Arctica, Antarctica have followed in succession. What will it be next, or will some of the old loves continue to claim our advances until full surrender?

The most prominent feature of geographical work since the last Congress has been the activity in Antarctic exploration. The international program formulated at the last two congresses has been carried out, and a large and valuable amount of work done and material secured.

England, Germany, Sweden, Scotland, Belgium, and France have all sent ships to this region, and the result has been to wonderfully increase our knowledge of that most interesting portion of the globe.

I shall not attempt any details or discussion. These we shall have first hand from those who have led the expeditions and been intimately identified with them.

In the Arctic field there has been continued activity.

Abruzzi, the able and energetic young Italian duke, has in a splendid and effective dash recorded the nearest approach to the Pole, and has by his experience eliminated Franz Josef Land from further consideration as a polar base.

Such type of young man, possessing already the prestige of a distinguished name, devoting his time, his abilities, his personal means to the advancement of human knowledge, instead of wasting them upon idle amusement, commands my highest admiration.

The expeditions of Sverdrup and Peary have returned from their four years' absence—one with a magnificent delineation of that previous great gap in Arctic charts, the unknown regions west of Ellsmere Land; the other with the delimitation of the northern terminus of the Greenland Archipelago, the most northerly known land in the world.

Mr. Ziegler, with commendable, but, I fear, misdirected persistence, is pushing his attack upon the Pole *via* Franz Josef Land, and news from his expedition may be received at any time. Amundsen is in the field laying siege to the north magnetic Pole.

But there remains still the Pole itself, and the mystery of that three million square miles about it, which stand as a challenge and a reproach to us.

In Asia, "the roof of the world," there have been numbers of workers.

The American explorers, Pumpelly and the Workmans, have done good work. The latter have attained the highest altitude yet reached by human beings, 7,135 meters.

But the magnificent work of Sven Hedin, the great Swedish traveler, far surpasses that of all other explorers in this region. In fact, this explorer undoubtedly stands foremost in energy and extent and accuracy of his work among the active explorers of the day.

Lhassa, "the Forbidden City," the mystery and secret of central Asia, the unattained objective of many travelers, has been reached and reported upon by several, and today the En-

glish military expedition of Captain Younghusband occupies the city. The sacred city of the Llamas is a mystery no longer.

In Africa, once "the Dark Continent," the work of large exploration is at an end, and has been succeeded by the work of division and colonization. No longer the "Dark Continent;" it is known in its geographical entirety better perhaps than South America.

The fine French surveys in the central Soudan, L'Enfant's determination of actual water communication between Lake Tchad and the Atlantic, through the Niger system, and young Grogan's feat, the longitudinal traverse of the continent from Cape Town to Cairo, are worthy of note.

Abyssinia in Africa, like Tibet in Asia, is being traversed and studied by travelers of various nationalities, and Ethiopia is emerging toward a place among the nations of the world.

In North America, "the granary of the world," numbers of explorers have been busy, more particularly in Alaska and the northern portion of the continent, but this work will be so well covered by various members during the meetings of the Congress that I shall not attempt it here.

A feature perhaps of this region has been the recent activity of the Canadian government in exploiting the northern lands, though more in a political than a geographical mood.

In South America the main work since the last Congress has been that of the government boundary commissions.

In Europe, "the metropolis of the world," geographical work is now of necessity a work of detail and rigid scientific development.

Of this class of work perhaps no better example can be given than that inaugurated and carried on by Sir John Murray in the Scottish lakes.

The papers before the Congress cover this work so well that I need to go no further.

In the domain of the oceans the material obtained in connection with the surveys for the Pacific cables and the development of the Pacific "great deeps" stand prominent.

So much for the work in the field, the work which by many is regarded as only the raw material.

As for the advances in the study, the laboratory, the class-room, the textbook, the list of papers before the Congress in the Departments of Meteorology, Technique, Bio-geography, Anthropo-geography, and Mathematical, Economic, Historical, and Educational Geography will attest.

What yet remains to be done? On this I can touch only in the briefest and broadest way, and from a personal point of view. The Congress will determine this question for itself during its sessions.

The fact of my personal interest in the polar field does not affect the truth of the broad statement that there is no longer any great pioneer work of geographical discovery to be accomplished except at the apices of the earth, at the North and South Poles.

Here alone large areas, guarded by the sternest natural obstacles to be found upon the face of the earth, still challenge and defy conquest.

It has been somewhat the fashion during the past few years, in the interest and enthusiasm excited for Antarctic work, to rather decry further Arctic work as not likely to be of value, and to assume that in the Antarctic region alone is there a field for really valuable scientific investigation.

I do not at all agree with this view. There are no 3,000,000 square miles of the earth's surface that do not contain scientific information of value much greater than the cost of securing it.

Further than this, I believe in doing the thing that has been begun, and that is worth doing, before shifting to a new object.

There is no higher, purer field of international rivalry than the struggle for the North Pole.

Uninfluenced by prospects of gain, by dreams of colonization, by land lust, or politics, the centuries' long struggle of the best and bravest sons of England, Germany, Norway, Sweden, Holland, France, Russia, Italy, and the United States, whose able delegates are here today, has made this field of effort classic, almost sacred.

The conquest of the Pole is a man's work as well as a geographical and scientific desideratum, and its attainment would move the man and the geographer in every one of you.

The South Pole, from a practical geographic point of view, is no less a prize (but I do not consider it a greater) than the North Pole, but the North Pole has a place in history, in literature, in sentiment, if you will, which the South Pole will never hold.

Granted the attainment of the North Pole, or that the attacks upon both can be carried on simultaneously, there is no greater believer or stronger advocate of the value and necessity for South Polar exploration and the desirability of pushing it to the very Pole itself than I.

I will note here but two other geographical feats of primary magnitude yet to be accomplished by the explorer.

The culminating peak of Asia remains yet to be won.

The culminating point of North America remains yet untrodden by human foot.

Large as has been the work done in the last nine years, the three salient resolutions of the Sixth and Seventh Congresses regarding Antarctic exploration, map of the world on a uniform scale, and oceanography still hold good, and I hope to see them reaffirmed by this Congress with a fourth in regard to Arctic work.

It seems to me we ought not to deny the advantages to science of *completing* the exploration of the Arctic regions, when the secrets of an area almost as large as Australia, an area within which a valuable paper before this Congress will indicate the probability of a new land, remain unknown.

And I sincerely hope that this Congress will not ignore a field of investigation which, now that the flood tide of Antarctic exploration has somewhat spent itself, resumes its leading place with five expeditions in the field or preparing to enter it.

The meeting of this Congress in this country holds great possibilities of good for us, both as individual geographers in being brought in direct contact with the work of our colleagues of other countries, who are hewing new paths and broadening old ones, and also as a country.

I earnestly hope that this session of the Congress will prove a great and lasting stimulus to the interest of our people in geographical and allied research.

We need a vigorous stirring up and awakening to the value of such work. With our abundant wealth, with our youth as a nation, our energy, push, ambition, and adaptability, yet as a country we have taken no part in large efforts in the geographical field for the past twenty years, but have allowed you, our friends across

the water, to shame us by your splendid examples.

There is ample room for a larger force of active, able workers in the field of geographical investigation.

There is too much money devoted to schools and libraries and too little to the field of exploration and research, which furnishes the facts for instruction in the schools and material with which to fill the volumes in the libraries.

I sincerely hope that the stimulus of this Congress, the breadth and strength of the resolutions which it may pass, and the union here at this Congress, for a common object, of all the American Geographical Associations, all combined, will lead to such a general interest as will enable us to take up some broad scheme of exploration and investigation and pursue it systematically and persistently, not capriciously and spasmodically, to its ultimate end.

Personally I should like to see such an interest aroused as would enable us to take up Antarctic exploration, which our friends across the water have so splendidly begun and prosecuted for the last four years, and which I judge they will not pursue further at present, and with the advantage of their advice and experience, carry it steadily forward.

The whole history of Antarctic and Arctic exploration has been a series of eager spasmodic efforts, attaining a greater or less measure of success, accompanied in many instances by semi-frantic and lavish rescue expeditions, necessary in some instances, not necessary in others, followed by a reaction and apathy till the training and experience gained is forgotten, and a new generation, making another attempt, must begin all over again.

This is not the way. Such spasmodic efforts will never do the work in the way science today demands. There must be continuous work extending over a series of years. The project should be taken up with the understanding that it must be carried on steadily for five or ten or more years; it must be handled like any humdrum business proposition; it must be divested of any sensational tendency.

The idea that as soon as a party enters the Arctics or Antarctic circle preparations must begin for the rescue must be thrown to the winds.

The loss of a ship or a few men must be discounted.

Such things happen every day in the maritime world, but it does not keep other ships and men from continuing the same voyages.

The world is getting bigger and wealthier every day.

There are abundant means seeking new avenues of expenditures if only they can be interested. It is a time of big things. Our friends over the water have shown us an example in their munificent Antarctic Expedition.

If our geographical societies and scientific institutions and the government would unite, such scheme of work could be carried on at an annual expense not more than a quarter or a fifth of the annual income of some of our great institutions.

I have taken Antarctic exploration as an example. Personally I should prefer to see that carried out, but it might just as well be the continued systematic study of the ocean on a large scale.

The point I want to make is that the time is ripe, and we should have some broad national project of geographical investigation, of general interest and coördinated plan, on a continuing basis, instead of frittering away of time and money on a heterogeneous variety of investigations of narrow scope and often of small value.

That there are other fields of investigation of great value and promise within the domain of this Congress goes without saying. Recognized specialists in these fields will bring them to the attention of the Congress in their own masterly way.

I have spoken upon those things upon which I think and feel strongly.

In conclusion, I wish to express our obligations and acknowledgments to His Excellency President Roosevelt, that splendid, vigorous, typical American, who stands at our head today, the fearless, unhesitating man of magnificently wedded thought and action, who has graciously consented to head the Congress;

To Baron Richthofen and his colleagues of the Executive Committee of the Seventh International Geographic Congress, for the way in which they have carried out the work intrusted to them by that Congress;

To our distinguished foreign visitors and friends, who have devoted so much time and effort to be present;

To those who, prevented by circumstances from being present in person, have sent us most valuable papers;

To Professor McGee and his colleagues of the Committee of Arrangements; and

To Professor Davis and his colleagues of the Committee on Scientific Program, for their tireless efforts in behalf of this Congress.

I cannot close without a word or two expressing my deep appreciation of the honor shown me in electing me President of this distinguished organization, a position previously held by such eminent men as De Lesseps, Ser-moneta, Gobat, Markham, and Richthofen.

I have accepted the honor in the spirit in which I believe it was tendered, namely, as an expression of the sympathy and approval of the geographers and geographical associations of this country and their interest in the work and aims with which I have been identified for the past fifteen years.

As such, I greatly prize it.

Further, I deeply regret that insistent press of that same work has made it impossible for me to labor for the Congress as I should have done.

The full and entire credit for the Congress, both in scope and detail, is due to the able and tireless chairmen and members of the Committees of Arrangements and Scientific Program and their associates, and to the delegates and members who have contributed the progeny of their brains to make it a success.

COMMANDER PEARY'S NEW VESSEL

THE steamship which has been especially built for Commander Peary's Arctic expedition was launched on March 23. Mr. Peary appropriately named her *Roosevelt*, in acknowledgment of the great interest taken by the President in polar work.

The vessel is described as a "three-masted fore-and-aft schooner-rigged steamship, with auxiliary sail power." Her principal dimensions are: Length over all, 182 feet; beam, 35.5 feet; depth, 16.3 feet; mean draft with stores, 17 feet; gross tonnage, 614 tons, and estimated displacement about 1,500. Her model is similar to modern-built steam whalers, but rather more sharp, the particular features being her long, high, raking bow, overhanging stern, and general wedge shape at the sides, in order that she may be lifted free if nipped in the ice.

The steamship was built of white oak, the frames being treble and close together, with double planking, making the walls from 24 to 30 inches thick. The keel is 16 inches thick, but false keels and keelsons form a backbone projecting 6 feet under the entire length of the vessel. The bow is backed by 12 feet of solid dead wood. Her engine and boilers will develop 1,000 to 1,500 horse-power. Her cost when ready for sea will be $100,000. The funds for the vessel's construction were supplied by the Peary Arctic Club of New York.

Vol. XVII, No. 11   WASHINGTON   November, 1906

FARTHEST NORTH

AS this number goes to press news is received of Peary's success in reaching the "Farthest North," 87° 6′. Our information is limited to the brief telegrams printed below, but they tell enough to show that the latest expedition of Peary has been the most successful he has yet made. The public will probably be most interested in the fact that Peary has won back for America the record of the farthest north, held by Nansen and Abruzzi since 1896. Previous to Nansen's voyage, America had held the record for 14 years by reason of the achievement of Lockwood and Brainerd, of the Greely expedition, in reaching 83° 24′.

Peary's first telegram was as follows:

> "Hopedale, Labrador,
> "Via Twillingate, Newfoundland,
>   "*November 2*, 1906.
> "*Secretary Herbert L. Bridgman, Peary Arctic Club:*
> "*Roosevelt* wintered north coast Grant Land, somewhat north Alert's winter quarters. Went north with sledges February via Hecla and Columbia. Delayed by open water between 84 and 85 degrees. Beyond 85 a six days' gale disrupted ice, destroyed caches, cut off communication with supporting parties, and drifted east. Reached 87 degrees 6 minutes

N. latitude over ice drifting steadily eastward. Returning ate dogs. Drifted eastward, delayed by open water. Reached north coast Greenland in straitened conditions. Killed musk oxen and returned along Greenland coast to ship. Two supporting parties driven on north coast Greenland. One rescued by me in starving condition. After one week's recuperation on *Roosevelt* seldged west, completing north coast Grant Land, and reached other land near 100th meridian. *Roosevelt* magnificent ice fighter and sea boat. No deaths or illness in expedition.

> "Peary."

A more detailed account of the new land which Peary reports he has discovered near the 100th meridian is awaited with much interest. There are many possibilities connected with this new land. It may be simply a small island or it may be a large body of land extending considerably northward, and thus afford future explorers opportunity to carry their base nearer to the Pole than has been possible in the past. In the June, 1904, number of the National Geographic Magazine, Dr. R. A. Harris, of the U. S. Coast and Geodetic Survey, who had been making a careful study of tidal records taken on the north coast of North America, argued that there must be a considerable body of land in the

COMMANDER ROBERT E. PEARY, U. S. N.

HERBERT L. BRIDGMAN,
SECRETARY OF PEARY ARCTIC CLUB

unexplored region to the north. He could account for the rise and fall of the tides there in
no other way. Dr. Harris outlined the supposed
land as extending eastward to about the 100th
meridian, and also to the Pole. Perhaps the land
Peary has found is this "supposed land."

Peary took his ship, the *Roosevelt*, further
north than any ship had previously been, and
passed the winter on the north coast of the most
northern known land. In every previous expedition Peary has been prevented from getting
his ship to this point because the channel
through which his ship must pass has every time
been choked with ice. As a result, he has always
been obliged to make his base far to the south
of his last base, which was only 500 miles from
the Pole. It has been generally believed that if

he could once get his base as far north as he did
last year, he would reach the Pole, for the four
great sledging journeys he has made in the arctics have averaged more than this distance to the
Pole and back. Open water and the drift of the
ice, however, prevented his advancing further
than 87° 6', which is 174 geographical miles, or
200.36 statute miles, from the Pole.

It is evident that Commander Peary is planning one more campaign against the Pole, for
he telegraphed Mr. Morris K. Jessup, the president of the Peary Arctic Club and its most generous patron, as follows:

*"Morris K. Jessup, president of Peary Arctic Club, from
Hopedale, Labrador, via Twillingate, N. F.*
"Steamer *Roosevelt* now here repairing rudder
and stern, taking ballast and awaiting arrival mail
steamer to secure coal. Return voyage incessant
struggle with ice to Cape York, September 26. Then

CAPTAIN SAM BARTLETT,
SAILING MASTER

SLEDDING SUPPLIES TO THE LAND

MAT HENSON, THE COMPANION
OF PEARY IN ALL SLEDGING TRIPS

storms and head winds to Labrador coast, October 13. Carried away two rudders, stern post, and two blades of propeller, foretopmast and spanker boom. Lost one boat, burned all coal and some interior beams, using wood and blubber along the coast.

"Expect to communicate again from Chapeau. Progress will be slow, but have no anxiety for our safety, and give no credence to exaggerated reports.

"*Roosevelt* is returning this year for additional supplies and for repairs. Several tons of whale meat dog food thrown away last fall after poisoning number of the dogs. Other supplies lost by the breaking of ice in April.

"PEARY."

Commander Peary's polar steamship, the *Roosevelt*, left New York on her long journey in search of the North Pole July 16, 1905. The *Roosevelt* was built in Maine, and was refitted at New York before starting. The vessel, for which funds were furnished by the Peary Arctic Club of New York, was designed particularly for arctic exploration. She cost about $100,000. The vessel has a crew of 20 men, under Captain Bartlett.

The best part of the last 20 years Commander Peary has given to Arctic work. He has mapped over 600 miles of coast line, measuring from headland to headland, without following the numerous deep indentations. Nearly half of it is entirely new coast line which Peary alone has seen.

He has proved Greenland an island and mapped its northern coast line; he has defined and mapped the islands to the north of Greenland, known as the Greenland Archipelago; he has shown that an ice-covered Arctic sea probably extends from the Greenland Archipelago to the North Pole; he has reached the most northerly known land in the world; he has gained the most northerly point yet reached— 87° 6′; he has studied the Eskimo as only one

can who has lived with them for years; he has added much to our knowledge of Arctic fauna and flora; of the musk ox, the Arctic hare, and the deer; the notes he has made during the past years will benefit meteorology and geology.

Aside from the satisfaction of having done a great and heroic work, there has been no material gain for Mr. Peary in these years devoted to Arctic discovery. He is known as one of the most talented men in the naval service, and if he had remained in active service would now probably hold a higher official rank than he does. Mrs. Peary, the devoted and able assistant of her husband's plans; Mr. Morris K. Jessup, and Mr. Herbert L. Bridgman, president and secretary of the Peary Arctic Club, share in large measure in the success of the expedition.

PEARY TO TRY AGAIN

MORRIS K. JESUP, president of the Peary Arctic Club, sends the Magazine the following statement:

The Peary Arctic Club, at its recent meeting resolved unanimously to place the *Roosevelt* on the docks for a complete outfit, and to thereafter tender the same to Commander Robert E. Peary for another attempt to be made by him to reach the North Pole. The club has taken this action upon reports furnished by Commander Peary, and believes that he will be successful. They have entire confidence in this gallant and intrepid American, and share in the pride which must animate the American people to see this effort, which the club believes will be the final one and the planting on the North Pole the American flag.

The steamer *Roosevelt* has not been structurally injured by the last voyage, and when repaired will be equally, and perhaps even more, able than when she started north in 1905.

The Peary Arctic Club asks the aid of those who have heretofore contributed, as well as the coöperation and aid of all or any who feel an interest in this patriotic enterprise. The expense of the expedition, it is estimated, will be one hundred thousand dollars, and it is hoped this amount will be contributed by the many, and not the few, as heretofore.

Subscriptions may be sent to President Henry Parish, New York Life and Trust Company, No. 52 Wall street, treasurer.

Morris K. Jesup,   President.

At a meeting of the Board of Managers of the National Geographic Society on March 7, President Willis L. Moore in the chair and the following members present, Messrs Charles J. Bell, Alexander Graham Bell, F. V. Coville, Charles Denby, A. J. Henry, C. Hart Merriam, General John M. Wilson, Gilbert H. Grosvenor, and F. B. Eichelberger, the following resolution, proposed by Dr. Alexander Graham Bell and seconded by General John M. Wilson, was unanimously adopted:

Resolved, That $1,000 from the Research Fund of the National Geographic Society be subscribed to the Peary Polar Expedition of 1907–1908.

In forwarding the amount President Willis L. Moore stated that the National Geographic Society wished to show its appreciation of the important scientific and geographical work performed by Mr. Peary during the past twenty years in the Arctic regions, and its hope that he may complete his explorations to the north of Greenland and Grantland by the conquest of the Pole.

NEAREST THE POLE

The substance of an address to the National Geographic Society
by Commander Robert E. Peary, U. S. Navy, describing his explorations in 1905–1906.

TO many persons, even of more than ordinary intelligence and wide reading, all Arctic work is an effort to reach the Pole.

To such the following facts will be of interest:

The incentive of the earliest northern voyages was commercial, the desire of the northern European nations to find a navigable northern route to the fabled wealth of the East.

When the impracticability of such a route was proven, the adventurous spirit of Anglo-Saxon and Teuton found in the mystery, the danger, the excitement, which crystallized under the name North Pole, a worthy antagonist for their fearless blood.

The results of northern efforts have been to add millions to the world's wealth, to discover some of the most important scientific propositions, and to develop some of the most splendid examples of manly courage and heroism that adorn the human record.

While these efforts have steadily circumscribed the area for new discoveries, they have also ripened the time for the final culmination of the work and the closing of the chapter.

Though the unknown area has steadily decreased, there is still ample room in the two or three million square miles of yet unknown area for startling surprises in geography and the natural sciences.

If any proof of this were needed, it is to be found in the directly contrary conditions found by the last Peary Arctic Club Expedition as compared with previous theories.

Many and perhaps all of my friends in this Society are aware that my last two Arctic expeditions have been financed by the Peary Arctic Club of New York, an organization composed of prominent men of New York, Brooklyn, Boston, and Philadelphia, with Morris K. Jesup as its President.

SCIENTIFIC RESULTS
OF THE LAST EXPEDITION

The point of view of Mr. Jesup and his associates in the club has been that Arctic work today should combine in intimate coördination two objects—the attainment of the Pole as a matter of record and national prestige, and the securing of all possible geographic, hydrographic, and other scientific information from the unknown regions about the Pole.

And since the government has not considered it advisable to undertake the work, the club gladly assumed it and shares the resulting honor and scientific material with the country and its museums.

What have been the results of this broad view?

To the popular mind has been given the satisfaction of feeling that the Stars and Stripes stand first, and that we possess a new world's record in a field in which the most enlightened nations of the world have been striving to emulate each other for three centuries.

To the geographer is given the satisfaction of having his horizon greatly widened in the western half of the polar basin; of being able to fill in annoying blanks upon his charts, and of looking forward with anticipation to detailed explorations of new land discovered. Added to this also is the definite determination of the insularity of Greenland—the arctic problem which Sir Clements Markham, President of the Royal Geographical Society, characterized as being second in importance only to the attainment of the Pole itself.

To the zoölogist comes the discovery of the beautiful white Arctic reindeer, ranging to the very limit of the most northern lands, from Robeson Channel westward to the one hundredth meridian, and the bringing home of a complete series of some fifty skins of this species; the securing of the first specimens of the beautiful salmon trout of Lake Hazen, and a wider extension of the known range and abun-

dance of the musk-ox, the Arctic hare, the fox, and the existence of animal life, as represented by seals, to the very highest latitude reached, within some two hundred miles of the Pole.

The oceanographer has for his share a new series of tidal observations, samples of the bottom obtained from soundings off more than half of the north Grant Land coast and down Smith Sound to Cape Alexander; a cross-section of the American outlet to the Polar Sea at its narrowest point, and new information in regard to the character and movements of the ice in the Central Polar Sea, resulting in the demolition of the paleocrystic sea theory.

For the glacialist there are the numerous inert or comatose glaciers of the North Grant Land coast which Aldrich took for snow-covered points of land, and the great glacial fringe of North Grant Land from Hecla westward, which when its features are known will appeal very strongly to investigators in this field.

To the geologist the discovery of fossils at Cape Hecla and at the most western point attained will be of interest.

For the ethnologist there is a new and complete census of the entire tribe of Whale Sound Eskimos for supplementing and comparison with previous censuses made during the past sixteen years; also additional photographs and measurements of these people, and an extension of the known range of their ancestors in the high northern latitudes.

To the practical explorer, particularly those who will yet wrest their final secrets from Arctic and Antarctic regions, the experience of the expedition, its freedom from sickness and death, especially scurvy, which has been the bane of so many expeditions, even up to some of the later Antarctic ones; its methods and equipment, its rapidity of travel, and its evolution of what I believe will be the type ship for Arctic and Antarctic work—able to fight or drift or sail equally well, as circumstances may demand—afford valuable lessons.

For the meteorologist have been obtained thermometric, barometric, and allied observations, carried on through what was undoubtedly a distinctly abnormal season.

In view of the above, and the fact that the work has defined the most northern land in the world, and fixed the northern limit of the world's largest island, was that work a useless expenditure of time, and effort, and money? Neither the club nor I think so. The money was theirs, the time and effort mine.

To the popular mind, and especially my enthusiastic friends of the press, the fact that the Stars and Stripes are in the lead is the one that appeals with instant strength; and I do not wonder at it, for they and you and I are aware that any record that represents a manly test of brains and body is a distinct asset to any nation; and they and you and I know that when the wires tell the world that the Stars and Stripes crown the North Pole, every one of us millions, from child to centenarian, from farm laborer and delver in the mines, up to the "first gentleman" in the land, will pause for a moment, from consideration of his own individual horizon and life interests, to feel prouder and better that he is an American and by proxy owns the top of the earth.

But the scientific results are the immediate practical ones, and British and foreign commentators do not obscure or overlook them; and these results together with the expedition's non-loss of a man, entire freedom from scurvy or sickness in any form, and return of the ship, have had their very friendly comments.

No better illustration of the practical way in which these business men of the Peary Arctic Club have approached the work and of our own practicality as a nation could be afforded than the quiet way in which the club's expeditions have set forth, and particularly the recent return of the *Roosevelt* as compared with the return of Nansen's *Fram*.

The latter came into her home port with salvos of artillery, a harbor covered with boats, and its shores lined with a cheering multitude, congratulations from King and Parliament; and Nansen today is Norwegian Ambassador to Great Britain.

The *Roosevelt* steamed into New York harbor, lay at anchor for forty-eight hours, and went to her shipyard for repairs without a ripple.

Do not for a moment get the erroneous impression that I speak of this in a spirit of criticism or complaint; on the contrary, I understand the situation fully and am entirely in accord with it.

We are too big to need to assert our existence to the other members of the family of nations, and things which to a smaller country might be the event of its life, to us are only one of several items in the day's work.

THE JOURNEY NORTH

In July, 1905, Commander Peary left New York in the *Roosevelt*, a powerful steamer with auxiliary sailing power, the first vessel to be built in America for Arctic work. He sailed north across the Gulf of Saint Lawrence, along the coast of Labrador, through Baffin's Bay to Smith Sound, on the northwest coast of Greenland. To that point it was summer sailing and child's play. Then the real work began. For the next eighteen days it was a continuous fight, through varying vicissitudes of open water and packed ice, 350 miles, to Point Sheridan, on the north coast of Grant Land, where the winter camp was made.

Arctic exploration expeditions must be made in two seasons. Through one summer the explorer must drive his ship as far north as possible, and then establish his base near to land before the six months' night sets in, in October. From then until the last few days of February, when the first glimmerings of the Arctic dawn are seen, the explorer must live inert in a darkness that is relieved only once a month by the pale light of the moon. Then, when light comes for an hour or less a day, he must start north by sledge.

This Peary did. Four parties set north, each with its sledges and dogs and Eskimo drivers and hunters. These Eskimos, with their dogs, the Commander said, are the factors that make the search for the Pole feasible. Two days' march brought Peary's party to a lead—a rift in the ice pack where open water prevents further progress. For six days the party camped at this lead, until a thinly forming shell of ice gave them a precarious passage to the northern side. Only fairly started north from here, they were entirely cut off from the three supporting parties by a blizzard which delayed them five days longer. From then on the diminishing amount of provisions and the serious delays demanded that one mad rush be made to the north.

The Commander's lecture was illustrated with excellent stereopticon views, which gave the audience a true idea of actual conditions in the far north. Great hummocks of jagged ice, precipitous pressure ridges and obstacles that would seem insurmountable, stood constantly in the way of progress. But they pressed on at a heart-breaking gait until on April 21 Commander Peary was forced to give the word to turn back. He had set a new record, but the Pole, on the reaching of which he had so firmly counted, was still 200 miles away—a distance he could have covered but for the sad delays caused by an open season and storms.

"At noon of April 21st we had reached a point which my observations showed to be in 87 degrees and 6 minutes north latitude, the nearest approach yet made to the Pole. It is perhaps an interesting illustration of the incongruity of human nature that at this time, when it might be thought that my feelings should be those of exultation only, they were as a matter of fact just the reverse. While I endeavored to be as thankful as possible for what I had accomplished, still the mere fact of breaking the record fell so far short of the splendid jewel to secure which I was straining my life out, that my feelings were of the intensest disappointment; and this, combined perhaps with the physical exhaustion resulting from our heart-breaking pace on half rations, gave me the deepest fit of the blues."

Turning south from his most northern camp, he traveled but a few days when, near the open water which had first intercepted him, he came across another lead from one-half to two miles wide. After camping two days and consuming almost all the few provisions left, pieced out by meat of weakest dogs, slaughtered because of dire necessity, a thin strip of ice was discovered across the lead. Over this, in skirmish line, each man fifty feet from his neighbor, they dashed, with the thin ice undulating under their feet and the danger of any moment sinking into the black waters of the Arctic sea constantly before them. No sooner had they landed on the firm ice of the southern side than the newly formed ice on the lead parted.

Emaciated men and starving dogs—only a few of the latter left—at last struck the coast of Greenland, with which Peary was familiar through previous trips. Here several Arctic hare which the Eskimos killed revived them slightly. Started on their first day's trip toward the west, they intercepted fresh tracks—three dogs and four men abreast, staggering as they went. Two runners sent east along this track returned in a day with Clark and three Eskimos, found as they had sunk down in exhaustion and despair to die a lingering and awful death.

For two days, with only short intervals of sleep, the party ate off the flesh of the muskox, seven of which Peary killed soon after reaching land. Then westward they went, until about June 1 the ship was reached.

FARTHEST WEST

Hardly recovered from the dash to the Pole, Peary started west along the north coast of Grant Land with a view to establishing some unknown coast lines. This journey took them west to the most northerly point of Grant Land, where a cairn was built and Peary's record and a strip of the American flag was deposited. This cairn is one of three such repositories which form a triangle of points established by Peary. One is on the most northerly point of Grant Land, and thus of the North American Archipelago; another is on the most northerly point of Greenland, and the third on the most northerly point in the world ever visited by man.

These three points, together with the explorations made by Nansen and Nordenskjold, make a fair investigation of the territory on the American and European sides of the Pole. The district lying north of eastern Siberia is the great unknown. What Peary terms the North American Archipelago is well explored as to coast lines, and but one strip remains unmapped on the northeast coast of Greenland. The Commander is absolutely confident that the Pole can be reached, this remaining strip explored, and perhaps a trip into the unknown toward Siberia made in one more journey to the north.

On return from the trip to the west Peary found that while his men had endeavored to change the position of the *Roosevelt*, she had become jammed in the ice and her rudder and two blades of her propeller torn away. With speed reduced by a damaged propeller and a temporarily rigged and extremely crude rudder, the *Roosevelt* started homeward, landing at Cape Breton, Newfoundland, November 23, 1906.

The stereopticon views with which the lecture was illustrated were remarkably good, and were a great factor in making the story clear and in elucidating the situation about the Pole. Pictures of the Eskimos were especially interesting, showing women with animation in their faces—a quality that seems to be absolutely lacking in the average pictures of these people. Laughing babies, dressed exactly as are their fathers and mothers, were shown, and one remarkable type of feminine beauty, the daughter of a chief with whom Peary had become acquainted during former trips to the North. Pictures of the animals which are found in the Arctic regions showed strange-looking muskoxen, a huge polar bear, large white Arctic hare, and some beautiful specimens of the snow-white Arctic deer.

IMPORTANT LESSONS
TAUGHT BY THE LAST EXPEDITION

The drift of the polar ice flow is constantly to the eastward. On the side of the Pole adjacent to eastern Siberia and Alaska is a great field of ice, whence the chilled air flows east to equalize the barometric pressure in the north Atlantic, where from the perennially open waters the comparatively warm air rises. This wind, blowing with a constantly varying intensity, drives the packed ice eastward, and the explorer traveling toward the Pole is as a man attempting to row across a river.

This drift is that on which Peary counts for success on the next dash to the Pole, but it is also that which carried him from his destination on his last dash.

Had the winter of 1906 been a hard one and the ice pack closed in the spring, it is the Commander's firm conviction that he would not have had to turn back when within 200 miles of the Pole, and it is his belief that, taking advantage of the experience gained on this last trip, not only can the Pole be reached when the next dash is made from the American side, but that the one remaining unexplored strip of Greenland coast can be mapped at the same time. The sledge parties should start in the next trip from a point much farther west than did his sledges, and should aim not directly at the Pole, but toward a point west of it, so that the drifting ice will carry the party to it.

It is not severely low temperature that is the obstacle to Arctic exploration. A sound man, properly cared for and properly clothed, should not feel that as much as we in the temperate zone do the sudden changes of temperature to which we are subject. It is the long winter night—a nerve-wearing experience, one which has driven men insane—and the necessity of carrying all provisions which make Arctic exploration perilous.

"The discovery not only of the North, but of the South Pole as well, is not only our privilege, but our duty and destiny, as much as the building of the Panama Canal and the control of the Pacific.

"The canal and the control of the Pacific mean wealth, commercial supremacy, and unassailable power, but the discovery of the Poles spells just as strongly as the others, *national prestige*, with the moral strength that comes from the feeling that not even century-defying problems can withstand us.

"Accept my statement, the attainment of the North and South Poles (the opposite ends of the earth's axis) by American expeditions would be worth to this country many times the few thousands needed, just for the closer bond, the deeper patriotism resulting, when every one of the hundred millions of us could say, 'The Stars and Stripes float at both ends of the earth's axis and the whole world turns about them.'

"Mere sentiment, perhaps; but sentiment has won battles and overthrown empires, and makes the difference between Satan and Saint."

PEARY'S TWENTY YEARS SERVICE IN THE ARCTICS

The following article is from "Handbook of Arctic Discoveries," by Major General A. W. Greely, U. S. A., and is copyrighted by the publishers of the volume, Messrs Little, Brown & Co., of Boston.

THE most brilliant work on the inland ice is that of Mr. R. E. Peary, U. S. Navy, who, in 1886, with a Dane, Maigaard, reached a point near Disco, some 50 miles from the sea.

Renewing his explorations in the *Kite*, Peary landed at McCormick Bay August, 1891, and most courageously persisted in his work, although his leg was broken while Crossing Melville Bay. A house was erected, but autumnal efforts to establish a cache at Humboldt Glacier were futile. In 1892 Peary, able to travel, explored Inglefield Gulf in April, and then turned to the accumulation of stores at the edge of the inland ice, some 15 miles distant. His main journey commenced May 14, when the true inland ice was reached with 16 dogs and 4 sledges. He crossed the divide of 5,000 feet elevation between Whale Sound and Kane Sea, and at a point 130 miles from McCormick Bay sent back Cook, who had supported him thus

far, with a man and two dog sledges. Peary proceeded with Astrup, and looked down into Petermann Fjord May 31; but crevasses here and at Saint George Fjord obliged them to make a detour to the east and southeast. Finally, on May 26, they reached the north edge of the inland ice, near 82° N., whence they looked to the north on the brown-red, comparatively ice-free land discovered by Lockwood in 1882. The fjord, into which they could not descend, doubtless connects with Nordenskjold Inlet of Lockwood, 1882, and Peary supports Greely's opinion of 1884, that Greenland here ends, and that the discovery of Lockwood is an entirely new land.

Unable to go farther north, Peary turned to the southeast to make the east coast of Greenland, and, following the edge of the ice-cap, reached Independence Bay July 4, 1892, and climbed Navy Cliff, 4,000 feet high, 81° 37′ N., 34 W. To the north was an ice-free land extending to the east some 50 miles, to 25° W. longitude; to the east and southeast the East Greenland Ocean was covered by disintegrating sea ice. Five musk-oxen were killed, which relieved anxiety for dog food on the homeward trip. The return journey to McCormick Bay, about 450 miles distant, was made almost in a straight line, the ice-divide proving to be 8,000 feet above the sea.

Believing that even more extended discoveries could be made in northeast Greenland by again crossing its ice-cap, Peary, raising funds for the purpose by a series of lectures, established a station at Bowdoin Bay in 1893. With 8 men, 12 sledges, and 92 dogs, he ascended the inland ice March 6, 1894, and in 13 days advanced 134 miles, to an elevation of 5,500 feet. Storm-bound by violent gales and extreme cold, Peary saw his dogs die and his men frosted, so that a general advance was impossible. Caching all surplus stores, principally pemmican, he sent back the disabled force, and with indomitable but fruitless energy marched on with three selected men. In 14 days he traveled only 85 miles, under extremely adverse conditions, being finally obliged to return with dying dogs and failing men. Abandoning sledges and caching pemmican, he reached Bowdoin Bay on April 15 with only 26 living dogs of the original 92.

Later his chief support, Astrup, sledged to Melville Bay and charted a considerable portion of its indefinitely located northeastern shore.

PEARY'S SECOND
CROSSING OF GREENLAND

When the visiting steamer *Falcon* arrived, in August, 1894, prudence demanded that the entire party should return to the United States. Food and fuel were insufficient, more extended explorations were improbable, and arrangements for a visiting ship in 1895 were merely problematical. With determination and courage bordering on rashness, Peary decided to winter at Bowdoin Bay with two volunteers, Lee and Henson.

Utilizing throughout the winter the entire resources of the region and gaining Eskimo recruits, Peary accumulated supplies on the inland ice, and started northward April 2, 1895, with his 2 men, 4 Eskimo, and 63 dogs, drawing 6 sledges. On the third march an Eskimo deserted with his outfit; but Peary, undiscouraged, pushed on. Most unfortunately, the heavy snows had obliterated all landmarks, and the expected mainstay—the pemmican cache—could not be found. Failure now impended, but, sending back his Eskimo allies, from this camp, 134 miles inland and 5,500 feet above the sea, Peary continued his journey, 41 dogs dragging the 3 sledges. The temperatures ran from –10° to –43°; the elevation increased to 8,000 feet; travel was bad; sledges broke down; Lee was frosted; dogs died; but Peary persisted on his hopeless journey. Finally, with but 11 exhausted dogs, 1 sledge, and a disabled man, Peary, May 8, left Lee camped 16 miles from the coast, and with Henson sought game ahead unsuccessfully for 4 days. Scant walrus meat reserved could barely feed their dogs during the home journey, but with desperate courage they advanced their camp to Independence Bay, Peary's farthest in 1892. The descent to the sea practically destroyed their sledging equipment; but 10 musk-oxen restored vigor to men and dogs. Further game failing, with 9 dogs and food for 17 days, they turned homeward in a frantic race against starvation. Twenty-five forced marches, in which necessarily everything but food was abandoned, brought them, in desperate condition,

June 25, to Bowdoin Bay, whence by the steamer *Kite* they reached Newfoundland September 21, 1895.

If Peary's advance beyond his buried cache was one of the rashest of Arctic journeys, yet the courage, fertility of resource, and physical endurance displayed by him and his companions place their efforts among the most notable in Arctic sledging. Other parties under less desperate circumstances have met with mortality, and only escaped total fatality by relief from their reserve party, which adjunct to Arctic exploration experience indicates to be essential to safety.

The two crossings of Greenland by Peary must be classed among the most brilliant geographic feats of late years, his journeys far surpassing in extent that of his ice-cap predecessor, Nansen, who crossed Greenland more than 1,000 miles to the south.

The physical collections and observations enlarge the previously existing wealth of scientific data of western Greenland. Doubtless the most important scientific results derived from the Peary voyages are those connected with Professor Chamberlin's examination of the glaciers of Inglefield Gulf, in which survey photography was freely used and to great advantage. Geology must profit from this study of glaciers presenting such varied forms, especially as the unusually free exposure of structure facilitated examination of vertical faces, convoluted and laminated formations.

The most attractive additions to knowledge are the ethnological studies of the Cape York Eskimo, which in 1895 numbered 253—140 males and 113 females. These studies, made by Peary, Lee, and Dr. F. A. Cook, appear in a memoir forming an appendix to Peary's "Northward Over the Great Ice" (2 vols., New York,

1898), though very interesting details are scattered through the general narrative.

In a summer voyage of 1896 Peary obtained and brought from the vicinity of Bushman Island, east of Cape York, two large meteorites. The following year he was fortunate enough to be able to obtain and bring to New York city the largest known meteorite of the world. It is an irregular mass, with maximum measurements of 6, 7.6, and 11.2 feet and weighs nearly 100 tons.

HIS FIRST CAMPAIGN TO REACH THE NORTH POLE

In June, 1898, he left New York for a four years' expedition against the Pole. His ship, the *Windward*, unable to force its way into Kennedy Channel, wintered near Cape Hawkes. In September of that autumn Peary determined the continuity of Ellesmere and Grinnell Lands. Through the utilization of the Etah Eskimo he planned to make Fort Conger his base for polar work. Adopting the unprecedented and dangerous policy of winter sledging, his trip to Conger in December badly crippled him and nearly cost his life, his feet being very badly frozen. Eight toes were amputated March 13, on his return to the *Windward*, yet he took the field in a few weeks. In July, crossing Ellesmere Land and passing over inland ice at an elevation of 7,000 feet, he discovered a fjord (Cannon Bay) running 50 miles to the northwest, with the north shore of Greely Fjord in the background, and probably Heiberg Land.

The *Windward* returning to the United States, Peary wintered (1899–1900) at Etah, from which he made his first northern effort. Leaving Etah in March, he started from Fort Conger April 11, taking the Greenland trail of Lockwood and Brainard. May 8 Peary passed

Lockwood's farthest, 83° 24′ N., and reached the most northern land in about 83° 35′ N. Striking northward over the polar pack, Peary found "frightful going, fragments of old floes, ridges of heavy ice thrown up to heights of 25 to 50 feet, crevasses and holes masked by snow, the whole intersected by narrow leads of open water."

Finding that the pack was disintegrated, he turned back in May, 1900, from 83° 54′ N., nothing but ice being visible to the north from the summit of a floeberg 50 feet high. Following the coast of Hazen Land southeast to 82° 45′ N., 24° W., he turned back about 125 miles from Independence Bay.

Though the North Pole was not reached, yet the northern end of the Greenland Archipelago had been rounded and its eastern coast determined to Cape Independence. This journey practically completes the outlines of Greenland.

It is extremely interesting to learn that this northernmost land of the world is replete with animal and vegetable life. Bears, wolves, hares, and musk-oxen make it their habitat. Of the extreme northeastern coast Peary says: "It is inhabited by a fauna practically the same as that of other Arctic lands several hundred miles farther south."

The discoveries of Peary and Sverdrup confirm the opinion advanced by Greely, that the Eskimo, musk-ox, and wolf have reached east Greenland from the Parry Archipelago via Greely Fjord, Lake Hazen, and the ice-free regions of extreme northern Greenland. Traces of Eskimo life cover the greater part of the route, and Peary believes that summer would disclose others.

Returning south, Peary fixed his winter quarters at Fort Conger and attempted the Cape Hecla route in 1901, but the northern advance in April was abandoned at Lincoln Bay. His base was transferred the next winter to Payer Harbor.

Peary was not dismayed, and starting in February, 1902, by twelve wonderful marches reached Conger. Leaving, February 24, 1902, with nine sledges, he was stormbound a day at Lincoln Bay. In rounding Cape Henry he struck the worst ice-foot he ever encountered. By the slipping of a sledge two men nearly lost their lives, they dangling over the crest of an ice-pack precipice some 50 feet in height. The sledges had to pass a shelf of ice less than a yard wide, with the precipitous face of a cliff on one side and on the other sea-floes 75 feet below.

Peary, having already traveled 400 miles in a month, with temperature ranging from –38° to –57°, left Cape Hecla April 6 with seven men and six dog sledges. The disintegrating polar pack was constantly shifting, while its alternations of rubble, open water, young ice, and pressure ridges made travel slow and arduous in the extreme.

Strong gales not only kept them stormbound, but still further broke up the pack. Leads became frequent and wider, old floes broke up, and the moving ice-pack, crushing together with a sound of heavy surf, made the situation most dangerous. One lead was closed up by a huge pressure-ridge about 90 feet high. At the farthest, observations gave 84° 17′ N., 70° W.; magnetic variation, 99° W.

This notable northing, made from a base 300 miles south of the *Alert*, over Markham's route, exceeded his latitude by 57 miles. Peary surpassed the northing of Lockwood on Hazen Land by 53 miles, and so attained the highest latitude reached in the Western Hemisphere.

NO MAN'S LAND—SPITZBERGEN

THE discovery of Spitzbergen excited little interest at the time, but it was prominently brought to the attention of the world by the first voyage of Henry Hudson, in 1607, to discover a passage by the North Pole to China and Japan.

Hudson's voyage was of vast industrial and commercial importance, for his discovery and reports of the vast number of walruses and whales that frequented the seas gave rise to the Spitzbergen whale fishery. Enterprising Holland sent its ships in 1613, bringing in its train later whalers from Bremen, France, and other maritime centers.

The whale fishery, as the most important of Arctic industries—from which Holland alone drew from the Spitzbergen seas in 110 years, 1679–1778, products valued at about ninety millions of dollars—merits brief attention.

Grad writes: "The Dutch sailors saw in Spitzbergen waters great whales in immense numbers, whose catch would be a source of apparently inexhaustible riches. For two centuries fleets of whalers frequented the seas. The rush to the gold-bearing places of California and the mines of Australia afford in our day the only examples at all comparable to the host of men attracted by the northern fishery."

During the most profitable period of the Dutch fishery, 1620–1635, it is within bounds to say that over 300 Dutch ships and more than 15,000 men annually visited Spitzbergen; more than 18,000 men were on the coast in one summer, says Lamont. It is definitely known that 188 whalers congregated at one anchorage in

1689, and in 1680 the Dutch sent out 260 ships and about 14,000 men, who made a catch at nearly a million and a quarter of dollars.

In the year 1620 whales frequented the bays and immediate coast of Spitzbergen in such numbers that the fishers were embarrassed to transport homeward the blubber and other products. These conditions led to the summer colonization of Spitzbergen (and Jan Mayen), where establishments for trying-out, cooperage, etc., were erected, as the most economical method of pursuing the industry. They were occupied only in summer, although the experiences of Pelham and other English sailors, who involuntarily wintered in Spitzbergen in 1630–1631, led to an attempt to establish a Dutch colony. The party of 1633–1634 wintered successfully, but that of the following year perished, and so ended the experiment.

The most remarkable of these establishments was at Amsterdam Island, where on a broad plain grew up the astonishing village of Smeerenberg. Here, nearly within ten degrees of the North Pole, 79° 50′ N., for a score of years, prevailed an amount of comfort and prosperity that can scarcely be credited by the visitor of today. Several hundred ships, with more than 10,000 men, visited it annually. These consisted not alone of the whalers and land laborers, but of the camp-followers who always frequent centers of great and rapid productivity.

In the train of the whalers followed merchant vessels, loaded with wine, brandy, tobacco, and edibles unknown in the plain fare of the hardy fishers. Shops were opened, drinking booths erected, wooden (and even brick) tile-covered houses constructed for the laborers or visiting whalemen. Even bakeries were constructed, and, as in Holland, the sound of the baker's horn, announcing hot, fresh bread, drew crowds of eager purchasers. If report errs not, even the Dutch frau of 1630 was sufficiently enterprising to visit Smeerenberg.

The shore fisheries soon failed (about 1640) and, the Dutch being driven to the remote and open seas, Smeerenberg fell into decadence; the furnaces were demolished, the copper caldrons removed, and the tools and utensils of the cooper and whaler disappeared; only the polar bear remained to guard the ruins of the famous Spitzbergen fair.

But human interest in Smeerenberg did not pass away with its vanishing habitations, for on the shores of that bay rest the last mortal remains of a thousand stalwart fishers, who closed their lives of toil and struggle in view of the icy seas that had often witnessed their triumphs over the mighty leviathan of the deep. Storm-stayed and ice-beset no longer, their dust awaits the change and fate ordained by God's eternal laws.

Spitzbergen of recent years has been claiming greater attention. A coal deposit of considerable value has been found on the island, and it has become a favorite resort for hunters and for excursionists. It is known as "No Man's Land," as it belongs to no country, Norway and Sweden being unable to agree as to its possession. Last year about half a million dollars' worth of oil, furs, and eider-down were obtained from the island.

Some authority ought soon to take possession of the archipelago, for the game—such as reindeer, polar bears, ptarmigan, geese, ducks, and other birds, formerly so plentiful—is being wantonly exterminated. A party of tourists last summer killed more than 100 reindeer, leaving the carcasses where they fell and taking with them only a few of the finest heads and antlers. Eider-duck nests are robbed of eggs, which Norway on her northern coasts and Denmark in Greenland protect by law.

Danes Island, on the northwest coast of Spitzbergen, was Andrée's starting point in 1897, and here also Walter Wellman has established his headquarters.

ANDREE'S FATAL ATTEMPT

The most daring of all schemes of polar exploration was that urged and undertaken by S. A. Andrée, of Sweden. A member of the Swedish International Polar Expedition of 1882–1883 and an aëronaut of some experience, Andrée succeeded in commanding for his plan the active support of Oscar, King of Sweden, M. Alfred Nobel, and Baron Oscar Dickson. In 1896 his party passed several weeks at Danes Island, Spitzbergen, where they erected a balloon-house and failed to start, owing to adverse winds. Observations of the escaping gas showed quite conclusively that the flotation life of the balloon had been over-estimated. On his return Andrée had the balloon enlarged and improved, so that its impermeability and flotative powers were increased. With the gunboat *Svensksund* and tender *Virgo*, Andrée revisited Danes Island in June, 1897. The balloon-house had withstood the winter storms, and after the installation of the balloon all possible means were adopted to reduce to a minimum its daily loss of gas by permeation through the envelope. The plan looked to the flotation of the balloon some 800 feet above the sea by means of three attached heavy guide-ropes, each 900 feet long, to which in turn were fastened eight ballast lines, 250 feet long, with which it was expected by shifting the position of the guide-ropes to change the direction of the balloon. On July 6 a violent gale barely escaped wrecking both house and balloon. Finally, on July 11, the wind was favorable in strength and direction and everything was ready. The balloon, named *Ornen* (The Eagle), had its load of about five tons of food, ballast, freight, and men, and from measurements of escaping gas had a flotation life of about 30 days.

Accompanying Andrée were M. Strindberg and M. Fraenkel. At 2:30 p. m. the lines were cut, and the balloon ascended about 600 feet. Suddenly it descended to the surface of the sea, possibly owing to an entanglement of the guide-ropes, and then rose again as the ropes were cut or broken and ballast thrown out. The wind carried the balloon across the mountainous island of Vogelsang, making it necessary to rise to some 1,500 feet, whence it passed out of sight in an hour, below the northeast horizon. As the balloon had at its best a flotation life of 30 days, it is obvious that the report is erroneous of its appearance in Siberia 65 days later.

Three message-buoys have been found, all dropped by Andrée on July 11, the date of his departure, which furnish brief news of the course of the daring aëronaut. The latest was dated 10 p. m., at which time the balloon was in 82° N., 25° E. All were well, the weather fine, the balloon at 820 feet altitude, the direction towards N. 45° E., and the ice field below rugged. Beyond these buoys there have been found no traces, despite repeated search in various Arctic regions.

WELLMAN'S EXPEDITION

Spitzbergen has also been selected as the starting point of Walter Wellman's expedition to the Pole in an airship. On Danes Island, on the northeast coast of Greenland, he built last year an enormous shed in which to inflate his balloon, and established a large plant. He returned to Spitzbergen in June, taking his dirigible balloon, which has been considerably enlarged and equipped with more powerful motors than previously planned. The steel car suspended to the balloon has a promenade deck 50 feet long, and space to carry about 15 dogs to drag the sledges in case the party are obliged to abandon the airship. Mr. Wellman believes the airship can be kept in the air 20 or 25 days. Spitzbergen is 600 miles from the Pole, and the trip there and back he estimates will take about 10 days. It will be remembered that Mr. Wellman last year asked the National Geographic Society to appoint a representative on the expedition to take charge of the scientific work. Major Henry E. Hersey, of the Rough Riders and the U. S. Weather Bureau, was so delegated by the Society and has gone north again in this capacity. Major Hersey, on his return from Spitzbergen in the fall of 1906, sailed with Lieutenant Lahm in the International balloon race from Paris, and it was his knowledge of meteorology that won the race for the Americans.

ARCTIC EXPEDITIONS COMMANDED BY AMERICANS*

EXPEDITIONS for Arctic exploration by Americans cover only about half a century, during which period they have both illustrated the resourceful courage of Americans and produced results comparable with those of European voyagers.

The following list of American expeditions is presented as of interest to our readers, and with the hope that its omissions and imperfections may be supplemented, so that the NATIONAL GEOGRAPHIC MAGAZINE may ultimately present a complete list of American voyages for Arctic exploration. The arrangement is generally, though not strictly, chronological rather than topical, although American effort has been especially active in the waterways to the west of Greenland.

The earliest expedition, extending aid in the search for Captain John Franklin, in 1851–1852, was the squadron commanded by Lieut. E. J. De Haven, U. S. Navy, its most northern work being in Wellington Channel, about 78° N.

Then followed the expedition of Elisha Kent Kane, nominally in search of Franklin, in 1853–1855, via Smith Sound, where, in 1854, Cape Constitution, in latitude 80° 35′ N., was attained.

Commodore John Rodgers, U. S. Navy, commanded the first American expedition to

pass Bering Strait, reaching, in 1855, Herald Island, 71° 18′ N., 175° W.

In 1860–1861 Isaac L. Hayes reached, on the east coast of Grinnell Land, an indeterminate point, which has been placed as Cape Joseph Goode, in 80° 11′ N. Hayes and W. Bradford, in a summer voyage in 1869, reached with the *Panther* the vicinity of Cape York, Greenland.

ROBERT E. PEARY, U. S. NAVY

*The data for this article are very largely drawn from the exhaustive *Handbook of Polar Discoveries*, by General A. W. Greely.

MORRIS K. JESUP

President of the Peary Arctic Club
and Honorary Member of the
National Geographic Society

From 1860 to 1862 and 1864 to 1869 Charles F. Hall explored the countries northwest of Cumberland Gulf. He reached, in 1861, Frobisher Bay; 1865, Boothia, in 68° N., 89° W.; 1867, Igloolik, Hecla Strait, 69° 22′ N.; in 1868, Fury Strait, about 70° N., and in 1869, Tod Island, off King William Land. In the Arctic Expedition of 1870–72, Hall reached, in the Polar Sea northwest of Greenland, 82° 11′ N., in 1870, and 82° 09′ N. on land in 1871. To effect the relief of Hall's Expedition, the *Tigress*, 1873, under Commander, afterwards Ad-

miral, Braine, U. S. Navy, reached Littleton Islands, in 78° N.

The Franklin Search Expedition of Lieut. F. Schwatka, U. S. Army, and William H. Gilder, 1877–1879, thoroughly explored King William Land, reaching about 69° N.

The International Polar Expedition, under Lieutenant, now General, P. H. Ray, U. S. Army, took station, in 1881–1883, at Point Barrow, Alaska, in 71° 24′ N., 156° W.

Of the two Howgate expeditions, one, in the *Florence*, under Mr. Sherman, a meteorologist, visited Cumberland Gulf in 1877, while the other, in the *Gulnare*, commanded by Lieut. G. A. Doane, U. S. Army, reached Disco, Greenland, in 1880.

Commander George W. De Long, U. S. Navy, the first to explore the great Arctic Ocean to the north of Asia, 1879–1881, reached thereon 77° 36′ N., 155° E., in 1881.

In 1880 Captain C. L. Hooper, Revenue Marine Service, sailing on a summer voyage via Bering Strait, skirted the south shore of Wrangell Land,* about 71° 30′ N., 180° W., and landed on this island in 1881.

Commander R. M. Berry, U. S. Navy, in the Jeannette Relief Expedition of 1881, explored Wrangell Land to its northernmost point, in 71° 32′ N., about 180° W. In 1889 Captain, now Admiral, Stockton, U. S. Navy, reached Wrangell Land, in about 71° 30′ N., 180° W.

The Lady Franklin Bay International Polar Expedition, under Lieutenant, now General, A. W. Greely, U. S. Army, took station, in

*Wrangell Land was first visited by an American whaler, Thomas Long, who sailed along its southern coast, reaching 70° 46′ N., 180° W., in 1867, in which year it was also skirted by other whalers, Captains Bliven, Phillips, and Raynor.

A GROUP OF ESKIMO WOMEN

1881–1883, on Grinnell Land, in 81° 44′ N., 65° W. It attained, in 1882, 83° 24′ N., 41° W., on the northwest coast of Hazen Land. In 1883 it reached 82° 15′ W. on the northwest coast of Greenland, and also 80° 48′ N., 78° W., on Greely Fjord. The auxiliary expeditions of 1882, under W. M. Beebe, reached Cape Sabine, about 78° 30′ N., and that of 1883, under Lieutenant, now General, E. A. Garlington, U. S. Army, passed a few miles to the north of that cape, and Commander, afterwards Admiral, F. Wilde, U. S. Navy, reached that year the vicinity of Cape York, in the *Yantic*. The relief squadron of 1884, under Captain, now Admiral, W. S. Schley, U. S. Navy, likewise reached Cape Sabine.

Dr. Franz Boas explored Baffin's Land in 1883–1884.

The most remarkable series of American expeditions is that due to the repeated efforts of Commander Robert E. Peary, U. S. Navy, which, beginning by a journey of fifty miles on the inland ice from Disco, in 1886, has ended in voyages, from 1892 to 1906 (except in 1897), that have covered entire north Greenland, northern Grinnell Land, and the adjacent Polar Sea. The main points reached were as follows: 1892, crossing the inland ice to Navy Cliff, 81° 37′ N., 34° W.; 1893, half-way across the inland ice, to about 80° N., 50° W.; 1895, across the inland ice to about 81° 40′ N., 34° W.; 1896

AKATINGWAH
Wife of Ooblooyah, with baby

A STUDY IN BRONZE
The face of an Eskimo woman

(summer voyage), Cape York; 1898, Fort Conger, 81° 44′ N., 64° W.; 1900, Polar Sea, 83° 54′ N., 30° W.; 1901, Lincoln Bay, about 82° N., 63° W.; 1902, Polar Sea, 84° 17′ N., 70° W.; 1906, Polar Sea, 87° 06′ N., *which is the nearest approach to the north geographic pole.*

Connected with Commander Peary's explorations there were auxiliary explorations, which visited the Greenland coast between Capes York and Sabine. Among these were: In 1891 and 1892, *Kite*, R. N. Keely and G. G. Davis; *Falcon*, H. G. Bryant, 1894, which reached, in Jones Sound, 76° 15′ N., 82° W.; the *Miranda* under Dr. F. A. Cook, visited, in a summer voyage, Sukkertoppen, Greenland, in 1894, about 67° N.; *Diana* 1899, and *Erik*, 1901, H. L. Bridgman.

In 1894 Walter Wellman passed beyond Platen Island, north of Spitzbergen, reaching about 81° N. In his expedition to Franz Josef Land, 1898–1899, the latitude of 82° N. was attained by one party, while another reached 81° 26′ N., 65° E., on Graham Bell Island.

The Ziegler Expedition, commanded by E. B. Baldwin, in 1900–1901, reached Franz Josef Land, about 81° 30′ N.; that under A. Fiala, in 1903–1905, to Franz Josef Land, reached, in 1903, about 82° 04′ N. by sea. Auxiliary Ziegler expeditions in 1904 and 1905 were commanded by W. S. Champ, in *Fridtjof* and *Terra Nova*.

The expedition of Robert Stein to Jones Sound, 1899–1901, reached about 78° N.

A. P. Low, in the *Neptune*, after wintering in Cumberland Gulf, 1903–1904, reached, in the summer of 1904, Cape Sabine, Smith Sound.

There have been quite a number of Canadian expeditions, which, if not strictly Polar, were at least sub-Arctic. Among them may be mentioned the expedition of the Tyrrell brothers in the Barren Lands of Canada, 1893; the journeys of Dr. Robert Bell in the Hudson Bay region, and especially his explorations of south Baffin Land in 1897; the discoveries of Ogilvie in the Yukon and Mackenzie basins, and the voyages of Lieutenant Gordon, Low, and others to Hudson Bay. J. E. Bernier, in *Arctic*, reached and landed on Melville Island, 75° 06′ N., 106° W.

Walter Wellman established his balloon depot in 1906 at Danes Island, Spitzbergen, 79° 40′ N., and now returns to that station during the present summer.

EGINGWAH AND REINDEER AT CAPE HUBBARD

TYPICAL ESKIMO DOG

PEARY'S POLAR EXPEDITION

THE substantial and exceedingly generous subscription of $10,000 by Mr. Zenas Crane, of Dalton, Massachusetts, to the Peary Polar Expedition will probably enable Commander Peary to go north again in July, 1908. The *Roosevelt* has been refitted with new boilers and machinery and stocked with sufficient provisions for three years' absence. Provided $15,000 additional is subscribed, and we are informed by Commander Peary that he has good hope of obtaining this amount, the expedition will leave New York early in July. Commander Peary will take a second ship as far as Smith Sound to carry extra supplies and coal for the *Roosevelt*. After embarking his Esquimo at Etah, Greenland, he plans to force the *Roosevelt* as far north as the ship attained on his last expedition, and then to winter on the north coast of Grant Land, making his polar dash in the spring of 1909.

If Commander Peary can establish his winter's base for the coming expedition as far north as he had it last time, we have strong reasons for believing that he will succeed in reaching the Pole on the next attempt. His last dash across the ice was unsuccessful largely owing to the rapid current discovered by him setting eastward across the northernmost coast. This current, however, he intends shall help his advance on the present expedition, as he will march in a northwesterly direction instead of aiming straight for the Pole when he leaves land. The current would then carry him toward the Pole instead of away from it. Readers of this Magazine are referred to the special map of the North Polar regions and the Arctic number, July, 1907, which shows the route planned by Commander Peary for the present expedition.

It would be most unfortunate if sufficient funds were not forthcoming to enable Commander Peary to go north once more. He is in the prime of life and has more than twenty years of successful Arctic experience behind him. Mr. Zenas Crane merits the cordial approval of all Americans who want to see this great geographical problem solved soon and by an American.

TEN YEARS OF THE PEARY ARCTIC CLUB

By Herbert L. Bridgman

Secretary of the Club, Read at the Ninth International Geographic Congress, at Geneva, Switzerland, July 27–August 5, 1908

A LTHOUGH the Peary Arctic Club has not yet fully completed its work, it willingly improves the opportunity of the Ninth International Congress to place in the permanent records of geographical progress a brief résumé of its history and deeds for its first decade. The Club, unique and unprecedented in organization and methods, was the product of circumstances, and, though designed for a special field and a definite task, has a charter of broad powers and permanent value. Founded and brought into activity as an ally and resource of Commander Peary in his quest for the North Pole, it has demonstrated by ten years of continuous, unceasing labor the efficiency of its organization and the wisdom of personal responsibility and direct connection between cause and effect. When its present work shall be completed its legal and chartered powers will continue in perpetuity, and its experience and prestige may be made valuable assets to its successors, no matter in what field, in what lands or seas, they may choose to prosecute exploration and discovery.

The times were ripe ten years ago for the Peary Arctic Club. The new expedition, prefaced by seven years of successful work in Greenland, had been sanctioned by the geographical authorities; leave from the public service had been granted; the *Windward* was on her way from England, and the date for departure approached. Already Peary had four times traversed the inland ice-cap of Greenland, and in the judgment of both American and Royal geographers demonstrated its insularity—a judgment ratified by gold medals from each society; the three great meteorites, Dog, Tent, and Woman, had been brought from their cradles;

the Eskimo by kindness and humanity had been won to faithful and loyal alliance and, having had a year for preparation, were awaiting the arrival of their leader. The imperative need of the hour was an effective, responsible organization, which would provide the means and, not less important, organize and direct all the support and interest which might be developed among the American people. The original plan was twenty-five subscriptions of $1,000 each for four years, and with this list but partially filled, with the expectation that the vacancies would before long be made up and organization perfected, Peary sailed from New York July 4, 1898, on the *Windward*, and a few days later, accompanied by the auxiliary *Hope*, from Sydney, Nova Scotia. The ships parted August 12, off Etah, north Greenland, the *Windward* to winter in Allman Bay, the *Hope* to return to her home port, Saint Johns, Newfoundland. Both are now at the bottom, the *Hope*, lost in 1900, drifting helpless in a floe on a reef near the Magdalens, in the Gulf of Saint Lawrence, and the *Windward*, renewing the rôle of her early

COMMANDER PEARY'S SHIP, THE "ROOSEVELT"

The first American ship built specially for Arctic exploration. She is now northward bound for the winter quarters of Peary's expedition on the north side of Grant Land.

days, as a Dundee whaler, having been driven on a ledge near the Carey Islands June 15, 1907, sinking in the very waters which she had often traversed in safety. The *Eagle* (1886) and the *Falcon* (1892 and 1894), of the Peary ships, also lie now on the floor of the sea.

The subscribers supporting the expedition, upon which Commander Peary more than six months before had left for the North, met for the first time January 30, 1899—by chance, Friday—at 44 Pine Street, New York, and organized the Peary Arctic Club, electing as its president Morris K. Jesup, who held the office from that date until his death. A brief and succinct constitution was adopted, which set forth as the objects of the Club, "to promote and encourage explorations of the Polar regions, as set forth in Lieut. R. E. Peary's letter to the American Geographical Society, dated January 14, 1897, and to assist him in the completion of the geography of the same; to receive and collect such objects of scientific interest or otherwise as may be obtainable through Lieutenant Peary's present expedition, or other expeditions of like nature; to receive, collect, and keep on file narratives and manuscripts relative to Arctic explorations; to preserve such records and keep such accounts as may be necessary for the purposes of the association; and, further, to command in its work the resources of mutual acquaintance and social intercourse."

Contributors to the Peary Expedition of 1898 were constituted founders of the Club, and the approval of a majority of them was prescribed as a condition of future membership. Alfred C. Harmsworth, Esq., now Lord Northcliffe, was elected, in recognition of his gift of the *Windward*, an honorary member, the only one the Club has ever had, and after formalities had been completed the work of the ap-

proaching season was thoroughly canvassed. Clear and unanimous agreement was developed from the beginning that an auxiliary steamer should be sent north during the summer to communicate with Commander Peary, to take sufficient stores and material to meet any emergency which should arise, and to demonstrate that the support of the Club was practical and efficient.

Preparations were actively prosecuted, and on July 21, 1899, the *Diana*, in charge of H. L. Bridgman, Secretary of the Club, and Capt. Samuel W. Bartlett, as master, steamed out of Sydney, Nova Scotia, for the North, having on board nearly fifty tons of supplies and equipment, filling requisitions of Commander Peary. It was necessary to provide in the first place for the party of the *Diana* for at least a year, as her return, like that of all other Arctic-bound steamers, was uncertain; for the company of the *Windward* in case she should be met at the North, and to deposit for Peary and his party subsistence for at least two years. Nothing else would adequately meet the contingencies, which were further increased by the presence on the *Diana* of a party of Princeton University scientists, led by Prof. William Libbey and another sportsman, together with Robert Stein, of Washington, D. C., with two associates and supplies, who were landed at Payer Harbor, near Cape Sabine.

Etah was reached August 5, and on the next morning a characteristic letter and instructions from Commander Peary were taken from a bamboo pole, surrounded by rocks, on the summit of Littleton Island, the most northern post-office in the world. A week later junction was effected with the *Windward*, when her winter's imprisonment in Allman Bay and Commander Peary's midwinter marches along the ice-foot of

THE PRESIDENT BIDDING "GOD SPEED" TO THE INTREPID CREW OF THE "ROOSEVELT"

Fort Conger and his sufferings and disability from frost-bite were for the first time learned. The *Diana*, having gathered dogs and equipment from the native settlements and discharged her entire cargo on the rocky knoll of Etah, returned on schedule time to Sydney, and was followed a few days later by the *Windward* to Brigus, Newfoundland, where she was laid up for the winter.

Repairs having been effected, the *Windward*, with Mrs. Peary and Marie Ahnighito Peary on board, was dispatched in July, 1900, from Sydney a second time for the North, from which came that season no returning word. Therefore, early in 1901, the Club began to be-

stir itself to discover the fate of its leader, then almost two years isolated, and of the *Windward*, from which nothing had been heard since departure from Sydney. The former Hudson Bay steamer *Erik* was chartered, dispatched July 18, 1901, from Sydney, and on the morning of August 5 steamed into Foulke Fjord, where she found at anchor the *Windward*, which a few days before had broken out of her winter ice prison at Payer Harbor, with Commander Peary, Mrs. Peary and the entire party, American and native, on board. The following characteristic letter by Commander Peary, written on the chance that he might not meet the auxiliary ship, was delivered by him in person:

Conger, *April 4*, 1901.

My Dear Bridgman:

It gives me great pleasure to present to the Club the results of the work of 1900.

First. The rounding of the northern limit of the Greenland Archipelago, the most northerly known land in the world, probably the most northerly land.

Second. The highest latitude yet attained in the Western Hemisphere (83 degrees 50 minutes north).

Third. The determination of the origin of the so-called paleocrystic ice (floe berg), etc., etc.

Considering that I am an old man, have one broken leg and only three toes, and that my starting point was Etah, I feel that this was doing tolerably well. It is almost 1,000 years since Erik the Red first sighted the southern extremity of the archipelago, and from that time Norwegians, Dutch, Danes, Swedes, Englishmen, Scotchmen, and Americans have crept gradually northward up its shores until at last, through the instrumentality and liberality of the Club, its northern cape has been lifted out of the Arctic mists and obscurity. It seems fitting that this event, characterized by Sir Clements Markham as second in importance only to the attainment of the Pole itself, should fall in the closing year of the century. If I do not capture the Pole itself in this spring campaign, I shall try it again next spring.

My gratitude and respects to all the members of the Club.

Always most sincerely, Peary.

Six weeks later the *Erik*, after a desperate struggle with the ice, prevented from reaching headquarters at Cape Sabine, landed Commander Peary and his party on August 26 in a temporary camp, in Herschel Bay, Ellesmere Land, whence he later marched to headquarters, and, followed by the *Windward*, returned to Sydney late in September.

The next year, 1902, the *Windward*, having received at Newburg, New York, new engines and boilers, and commanded by Capt. Samuel W. Bartlett, entered for the third time the portals of Smith Sound, and on August 5, improving a fortunate few hours of open water,

succeeded in embarking, at Payer Harbor, Commander Peary, homeward bound after four years' absence, and reached Sydney safely, with his comrades of 1898, on September 15, closing the first chapter and the definitive obligations of the subscribers, the founders of the Peary Arctic Club.

A season of rest, but not of inaction, followed. The work of the *Windward* and her power, or rather lack of it, having been demonstrated in serious Arctic work, the steamer was sold early in 1903 to a Norwegian purchaser, who later restored her, for a consideration, to owners in her native Scotland. Commander Peary, having secured in September, 1904, further leave of absence from the service to prosecute and complete the work of his life, immediately began preparations for the construction of a ship which could meet the difficulties and could perform the service and could break down the barriers which had so far stopped advance to the North.[. . .]

Plans were made for a ship which should combine the necessary qualities of power, the smallest consumption, and the largest capacity for coal, of a model which should withstand shock and pressure, which should surmount and crush floes, which should respond on call with full power of engines—in short, a ship which should be the product of actual experience. The keel of the new steamer was laid late in the fall by Capt. Charles B. Dix, in a Bucksport, Maine, yard, and on March 17 the *Roosevelt*, christened by Mrs. Peary, was launched. Engines and boilers were installed at Portland in June, and on July 4, 1905, amid cheers and whistles and the waving of flags and signals, the *Roosevelt*, first American Arctic vessel for more than a generation, steamed out of New York harbor for the North.

Sixteen months later a wireless message informed the world that the *Roosevelt*, having wintered farther north than any ship in the Western Hemisphere, was at Hopedale, Labrador, crippled and short of coal, Commander Peary having attained 87.6°, a new "nearest the Pole," and all on board well. A month later, and after a slow, difficult, and laborious voyage, the *Roosevelt*, entering New York Harbor by its East River gate, was towed to her old anchorage at the foot of West Forty-second Street, and the expedition of 1905–1906 was ended.

Coincident with the construction of the *Roosevelt* and profiting by experience, the Peary Arctic Club was incorporated April 25, 1904, under the laws of the State of New York, with larger powers, greater efficiency, and other advantages. The definite business of the new organization, of which Morris K. Jesup, John H. Flagler, Anton A. Raven, Henry Parish, Herbert L. Bridgman, and Robert E. Peary were incorporators, was stated in the charter to be "To aid and assist in forming and maintaining certain expeditions to be placed under Commander Robert E. Peary, U. S. N., with the object of continuing his explorations of the polar regions and his completing the geographical data of the same; receiving and collecting such objects of scientific interest as may be obtainable through such expeditions; collecting, receiving, and preserving narratives and manuscripts relating to Arctic exploration in general; soliciting and administering funds for the maintenance of such expeditions, and in general providing funds for Commander Peary's efforts to reach the farthest northern point on the Western Hemisphere, and to cooperate with any other assistant for the same purpose."

It is not the purpose of this paper to speak in detail of the field work of the Peary Arctic Club; that belongs of right to the man who did it; but it may be proper to present here a brief résumé, or a statement of net results on the sea, ice, and land.

Fourteen times the ships of the Club have traversed boisterous Davis Straits, conquered Melville Bay, and established Sydney–Etah service with almost the regularity of transatlantic liners. The total mileage of these voyages, not including the fifteenth, upon which the *Roosevelt* is now engaged, would be probably not far from 50,000 miles, or sufficient twice to circumnavigate the globe; of the eight ships, one-half have met their fate (after passing out of the Club's service), but among officers and crews, more than one hundred in all, except the ill-fated *Falcon* and her company (also after her Arctic voyage was finished), no loss of life or serious accident has occurred.

A summary of the cruises of the Club's steamers is as follows:

1898. *Windward*, London to New York, to Allman Bay; *Hope*, Saint Johns to Sydney, to Etah, to Saint Johns.
1899. *Diana*, Saint Johns to Sydney, to Etah, cruise in Inglefield Gulf, to Sydney, to Saint Johns; *Windward*, Allman Bay to Brigus, N. F.
1900. *Windward*, Brigus, via Saint Johns, to Sydney, to Payer Harbor, Ellesmereland.
1901. *Windward*, Payer Harbor to Saint Johns; *Erik*, Halifax to Sydney, to Etah and return.
1902. *Windward*, Saint Johns to Newburgh, N. Y., to Cape Sabine, to Sydney, to Brigus.
1905. *Roosevelt*, Bucksport to Portland, to New York, to Sydney, to Cape Sheridan and winter quarters.
1906. *Roosevelt*, winter quarters, Cape Sheridan to Sydney and New York.
1908. *Roosevelt*, New York to Sydney and winter quarters.

Of the sledge and field work of the Club, it so far exceeds that of any other expedition that it may be fairly questioned whether it does not equal that of all combined. Six times along the ice-foot from Cape Hawkes to Fort Conger its sledges broke the way, until it resembled an open road, while Smith Sound, Robeson Channel, and Lincoln Sea were gridironed in all directions with their trails.

On the Greenland coast, delimiting for the first the northern boundary of this mysterious continent, it fixed Cape Morris K. Jesup in 1900, the highest northern land in the Western Hemisphere, and probably connected farther to the east the new land with Independence Bay, discovered by Peary six years before. The game located on this former journey also proved the salvation of the party upon their return from the farthest north, six years later. From Fort Conger north to Cape Hecla, from Cape Sheridan west, in the summer of 1906, the ice-foot afforded a path to the farthest west, whence the hitherto-unknown Crocker Land was visible, and the definite map of the Arctic Archipelago still farther extended.

Of the memorable sledge journeys across the polar pack, that of 1902, to 84.17°, highest north on the American Hemisphere, and that four years later to 87.6°, the highest north, the leader has the rightful prerogative of description; but they are recognized as among the major achievements of Arctic annals, not only in latitude attained, but in possession and exercise of those qualities which are the price of all Arctic success. The total number of miles covered by the sledges of the Peary Arctic Club during its ten years of field work is not less than 6,800 miles.

Additions by the Club to the nomenclature of Arctic maps may be summarized as follows:

1899:
  Jesup (Morris K.) Land.
  Moore (Charles A.) Mountain.
  Bridgman (Herbert L.) Mountain.
  Benedict (Erastus C.) Glacier.
  Hedin (Sven) Glacier.
  Cannon (Henry W.) Cape.
1900:
  Jesup (Morris K.) Cape, 1883–1890.
  Bridgman (Herbert L.) Cape.
  Parish (Henry) Cape.
  Wyckoff (Clarence F.) Cape.
  Hill (James J.) Cape.
  Cannon (Henry W.) Cape.
  Benedict (Henry H.) Mountains.
  Daly (Charles P.) Mountains.
  Constable (James M.) Bay.
  Wyckoff (Edward G.) Island.
  Schley (Grant B.) Fjord.
  Hyde (Frederick E.) Fjord.
  Sands (Hayden H.) Fjord.
  Peary (Mary) Peak.
  McKinley (William) Sea.
  Roosevelt (Theodore) Range.
1906:
  Crocker (George) Land.
  Phillips (John C.) Bay.
  Bourne (Fred. G.) Cape.
  Colgate (James C.) Cape.
  Hubbard (Thomas H.) Cape.
  Kleybolte (Rudolph) Island.

In addition to its definite work on the map of the world, the Peary Arctic Club was accomplished other things hardly less important and significant. It has demonstrated the indisputable value of the Eskimo and his dog; has substituted for strained relations, friendship and loyalty, sympathy with the leader and obedience to him, so that the undertaking commands the best resources of both races; each supplements the other, and the result has demonstrated the merit of the combination. The Club has also vastly simplified the equipment and dietary of explorers; has carried far beyond any former example the rule of "living off the country." Scurvy and other evils which enfeebled and reduced earlier explorers have been practically unknown, and, utilizing the abundant supplies of the food of the country, combined with the essentials, pemmican and tea from civilization, have demonstrated what is probably the ideal Arctic food supply. Starvation upon a selected basis has been practically eliminated from the Arctic dangers.

The Peary Arctic Club has also demonstrated the advantage of a small, compact organization with direct personal responsibility, free from routine "red tape" or the semblance, without the fact, of authority. Animated by absolute sincerity of purpose, by undivided earnestness in its one great object, it believes that its example in fields of administration and coöperation are not less instructive than its achievements in the field are gratifying.

Death removed from the Club, on January 22, 1908, Morris K. Jesup, its first and only president. To Mr. Jesup more than to any other man the Club owed existence, and from him it received in generous measure support, counsel, and inspiration, which sustained its work and commanded for it a definite place in public confidence and respect.

The vacancy caused by Mr. Jesup's death was filled June 18, 1908, by the election of Gen. Thomas H. Hubbard, of New York, and that in the vice-presidency, by the resignation of Commander Peary, on account of his approaching departure for the North, by the election of Zenas Crane, of Dalton, Massachusetts.

The Club's steamer *Roosevelt*, fully repaired, equipped with new boilers, stronger and better than ever, left New York for the North, a second time, July 6, 1908; and, having been honored at Oyster Bay, New York, by a visit from President Roosevelt, departed from Sydney July 17, upon a quest the complete success of which the Club confidently expects Commander Peary will report in person to the Tenth International Geographic Congress.

THE DISCOVERY OF THE POLE

W E print herewith the reports of Dr. F. A. Cook and Commander Robert E. Peary announcing the discovery of the North Pole April 21, 1908, and April 6, 1909. Before the National Geographic Society can, however, accept the conclusions of either Commander Peary or Dr. Cook that the North Pole has been attained, it will be necessary that the scientific records and data of each explorer be carefully examined by its Committee on Research or by some body or commission acceptable to the Board. The Society takes this position not from any distrust of the personal integrity of either explorer, but because of the many calculations that enter into the determination of the pole. The National Geographic Society urges Commander Peary and Dr. Cook speedily to submit all their observations, notes, and data to a competent scientific commission in the United States.

First Report by Dr. Frederick A. Cook, Sept. 1, 1909

A FTER a prolonged fight against famine and frost we have at last succeeded in reaching the North Pole.

A new highway, with an interesting strip of animated nature, has been explored.

Big game haunts were located which will delight the sportsman and extend the Eskimo horizon.

Land has been discovered upon which rest the earth's northernmost rocks.

A triangle of 30,000 square miles has been cut out of the terrestrial unknown.

The expedition was the outcome of a summer cruise in Arctic seas. The yacht *Bradley* arrived at the limits of navigation in Smith Sound late in August, 1907. Here conditions were found favorable to launch a venture for the pole.

Mr. John R. Bradley liberally supplied from the yacht suitable provisions for local use, and my own equipment for emergencies served well for every purpose of Arctic travel.

Many Eskimos had gathered on the Greenland shores at Annootok for the winter bear hunt. Immense caches of meat had been gathered. About the camp were plenty of strong dogs.

The combination was lucky, for there was good material for an equipment, expert help, and an efficient motor force, and all that was required was conveniently arranged at a point only 700 miles from the boreal center.

A house and workshop was built of packing boxes. The willing hands of this northernmost tribe of 250 people were set to the problem of devising a suitable outfit, and before the end of the long winter night we were ready for the enterprise.

Plans were matured to force a new route over Grinnell Land and northward along its west coast out on the polar sea.

Soon after the polar midnight the campaign opened. A few scouting parties were sent over to the American shores to explore a way and to seek game haunts.

Their mission was only partly successful, because storms darkened the January moon.

At sunrise of 1908 (February 19) the main expedition embarked for the pole. Eleven men and 103 dogs, drawing 11 heavily loaded sledges, left the Greenland shore and pushed westward over the troubled ice of Smith Sound.

The gloom of the long night was relieved by only a few hours of daylight. The chill of winter was felt at its worst.

As we crossed the heights of Ellesmere Sound to the Pacific slope the temperature sank to 83 degrees below zero Fahrenheit. Several dogs were frozen, and the men suffered severely, but we soon found game trails along which an easy way was forced through Nansen Sound to the land's end.

In this march were procured 101 musk oxen, 7 bears, and 335 hares, and then we pushed out into the polar sea from the southern point of Heiberg Island.

On March 17 six Eskimos returned from here, with four men and forty-six dogs, moving supplies for eighty days.

The crossing of the circumpolar pack was begun three days later. Two other Eskimos, forming the last supporting party, returned. The trains had now been reduced by the survival of the fittest. Etukishook and Ahwelah, the two best men, and twenty-six dogs were picked for the final dash. There was before us an unknown line of 460 miles to our goal.

The first days prevented long marches, and with encouraging progress the big lead which separated the land ice from the central pack was crossed with little delay.

Low temperature and persistent winds made life a torture, but, cooped in snow houses, eating dried beef and tallow and drinking hot tea, some animal comforts were occasionally to be gained.

For several days after the sight of known land was lost the overcast skies prevented an accurate determination of our positions.

On March 30 the horizon was partly cleared of its smoky agitation, and over the western mist was discovered a new land.

The observations gave our position latitude 84 deg. 17 min., longitude 86 deg. 36 min.

The urgent need of rapid advance on our main mission did not permit a detour to explore the coast.

Here were seen the last signs of solid earth. Beyond there was nothing stable, and even on scaling nothing was noted to mark the terrestial polar solidity.

We advanced steadily over the monotony of a moving sea of ice.

We now found ourselves beyond the range of all life. Neither the footprints of bears nor the blowholes of seals were detected. Even the microscopic creatures of the deep were no longer under us.

The maddening influence of the shifting desert of frost became almost unendurable in the daily routine. The surface of the pack offered less and less trouble. The weather improved, but still there remained a light life-sapping wind, which drove despair to its lowest recess.

Under the lash of duty, however, interest was forced, while the merciless drive of extreme cold enforced physical action.

Thus, day after day, the weary legs were spread over big distances.

The incidents and the positions were recorded, but the adventure was promptly forgotten in the mental bleach of the next day's effort.

The night of April 7 was made notable by the swing of the sun at midnight over the northern ice.

Sunburns and frost-bites were now recorded on the same day, but the double days of glitter infused quite an incentive into our life of shivers.

Observations on April 8 placed our camp at latitude 86 deg. 36 sec., longitude 94 deg. 2 sec.

In spite of what seemed like long marches, we had advanced but a little more than 100 miles in nine days.

Much of our hard work was lost in circuitous twists around troublesome pressure lines and high, irregular fields of very old ice.

The drift, too, was driving eastward with sufficient force to give some anxiety, though we were still equal to about fifteen miles daily.

The extended marches and the long hours of travel with which fortune had favored us earlier were no longer possible.

We were now about 200 miles from the pole and the sled loads were reduced. One dog after another had gone into the stomachs of his hungry survivors until the teams were considerably reduced, but there seemed to remain a sufficient balance of man and brute to push along into the heart of the mystery to which we had set ourselves.

Beyond the eighty-sixth parallel the ice-fields became more extensive and heavier, the crevices fewer and less troublesome, with little or no crushed ice thrown up as barriers.

From the eighty-seventh to the eighty-eighth, much to our surprise, was the indication of land ice.

For two days we traveled over ice which resembled a glacial surface. The usual sea ice lines of demarkation were absent and there were no hummocks or deep crevices.

There was, however, no perceptible elevation and no positive sign of land or sea.

Observations on the 14th gave latitude 88 deg. 21 min. and longitude 95 deg. 52 min.

We were now less than one hundred miles from the pole.

The pack was here more active, but the temperature remained 40 below zero, cementing together quickly the new crevices.

Young ice spread on the narrow spaces of open water so rapidly that little delay was caused in crossing from one field to another.

The time had now arrived to muster energy for the last series of efforts.

In the enforced effort every human strand was strained, and at camping time there was no longer sufficient energy to erect a snow shelter, though the temperature was still very low.

The silk tent was pressed into service and the change proved agreeable. It encouraged a more careful scrutiny of the strange world into which fate had pressed us.

Signs of land were still seen every day, but they were deceptive illusions or a mere flight of fancy.

It seemed that something must cross the horizon to mark the important area into which we were pushing.

When the sun was low the eye ran over the moving plains of color to dancing horizons. The mirages turned things topsy turvy. Inverted mountains and queer objects ever rose and fell in shrouds of mystery, but all of this was due to the atmospheric magic of the midnight sun.

Slowly but surely we neared the turning point. Good astronomical observations were daily procured to fix the advancing stages.

The ice steadily improved, but still there was a depressing monotony of scene, and life had no pleasures, no spiritual recreation, nothing to relieve the steady physical drag of chronic fatigue.

But there came an end to this as to all things. On April 21 the first corrected altitude of the sun gave 89 deg. 59 min. 46 sec.

The pole, therefore, was in sight.

We advanced the fourteen seconds, made supplementary observations and prepared to stay long enough to permit a double round of observations.

Etukishook and Ahwelab were told that we had reached the "Neig Nail" and they sought to celebrate by an advance of savage joys.

At last we had pierced the boreal centre and the flag had been raised to the coveted breezes of the North Pole.

The day was April 21, 1908. The sun indicated local noon, but time was a negative problem, for here all meridians meet.

With a step it was possible to go from one part of the globe to the opposite side.

From the hour of midnight to that of midday the latitude was 90, the temperature 38 and the barometer 29.83.

North, east and west had vanished. It was south in every direction, but the compass pointing to the magnetic pole was as useful as ever.

Though overjoyed with the success of the conquest, our spirits began to descend on the following day. After all the observations had been taken with a careful study of the local conditions a sense of intense loneliness came with the further scrutiny of the horizon.

What a cheerless spot to have aroused the ambition of man for so many ages!

An endless field of purple snows. No life. No land. No spot to relieve the monotony of frost. We were the only pulsating creatures in a dead world of ice.

We turned our backs to the pole on April 23 and began the long return march. Counting on a continued easterly drift, the course was forced further west.

With fair weather, good ice and the inspiration of the home run, long distances were at first quickly covered.

Below the eighty-seventh parallel the character of the ice changed very much, and it became evident that the season was advancing rapidly.

With a good deal of anxiety we watched the daily reduction of the food supply.

It now became evident that the crucial stage of the campaign was to be transferred from the taking of the pole to a final battle for life against famine and frost.

The clear blue of the skies changed to a steady, dismal gray. Several days of icy despair followed each other in rapid succession.

There were some violent gales, but usually the wind did not rise to the full force of a storm.

With starvation as the alternative, we could not wait for better weather.

Some advance was made nearly every day, but the cost of the desperate effort pressed life to the verge of extinction.

On May 24 the sky cleared long enough to give us a set of observations.

We had reached the eighty-fourth parallel near the ninety-seventh meridian. The ice was much broken and drifted eastward, leaving many open spaces of water.

There remained on our sleds scarcely enough food to reach our caches on Nansen Sound unless we averaged fifteen miles daily. With the disrupted "lalack" and reduced strength we were hardly equal to ten miles daily.

Trying to make the best of our hard lot, a straight course was set for the musk ox lands of the inner crossing.

At the eighty-third parallel we found ourselves to the west of a large tract, extending southward. The ice changed to small fields. The

temperature rose to zero and a persistent mist obscured the heavens.

The events of the following day were pressed into desperate action.

With a few lines on paper to register the life of suffering, the food for man and dog was reduced to a three-quarter ration, while the difficulties of ice travel rose to disheartening heights.

At the end of a struggle of twenty days through thick fog the sky cleared and we found ourselves far down in Crown Prince Gustav Sea, with open water and impossible small ice as a barrier between us and Heiberg Island.

In the next few days bears came along as life savers. The empty stomachs were spread and the horizon, for a time, was cleared of trouble.

With the return to Annootok rendered difficult by the unfortunate westerly drift, we now sought to follow the ice movement south to Lancaster Sound, where we hoped to reach a Scottish whaler.

Early in July further southward progress became impossible, and in quest of food we crossed the Firth of Devon into Jones Sound.

The dogs were here given the freedom of their wolf propensities, and by folding boat and sled we tried to reach Baffin's Bay. With but an occasional bird to eat and a long line of misfortune we pushed eastward until the frost of early September stopped progress.

With neither food, fuel nor ammunition we were forced to wrest winter supplies from what seemed at first like a lifeless desert.

Pressed by hunger, new implements were shaped, and Cape Sparbo was picked as a likely place to find life.

Game was located with the bow and arrow, the line, the lance and the knife. The musk ox, bear and wolves yielded meat, skins and fat.

An underground den was prepared, and in it we remained until sunrise of 1909.

On February 18 the start was made for Annootok. With a newly prepared equipment the Greenland shores were reached on April 15.

Here we were greeted by Harry Whitney and an anxious group of Eskimo friends.

To facilitate an early return I moved southward to the Danish settlement and reached Upernavik on May 21, 1909.

FIRST REPORT BY
COMMANDER ROBERT E. PEARY, U. S. N.,
SEPTEMBER 6, 1909

THE steamer *Roosevelt*, bearing the North Polar expedition of the Peary Arctic Club, parted company with the *Erik* and steamed out of Etah Fiord late in the afternoon of August 18, 1908, setting the usual course for Cape Sabine. The weather was dirty, with fresh southeasterly winds. We had on board twenty-two Eskimo men, seventeen women, and ten children, two hundred and twenty-six dogs, and some forty-odd walrus.

We encountered the ice a short distance from the mouth of the harbor, but it was not closely packed and was negotiated by the *Roosevelt* without serious difficulty. As we neared Cape Sabine the weather cleared somewhat, and we passed close by Three Voort Island and Cape Sabine, easily making out with the naked eye the house at Hayes Harbor occupied by me in the winter of 1901–'2.

From Cape Sabine north there was so much water that we thought of setting the lug sail before the southerly wind; but a little later appearance of ice to the northward stopped this. There was clean open water to Cape Albert, and from there scattered ice to a point about abreast of Victoria Head, thick weather and dense ice bringing us some ten or fifteen miles away.

From here we drifted south somewhat, and then got a slant to the northward out of the current. We worked a little further north, and stopped again for some hours. Then we again worked westward and northward till we reached a series of lakes, coming to a stop a few miles south of the *Windward*'s winter quarters at Cape Derville.

From here, after some delay, we slowly worked away northeastward through fog and broken ice of medium thickness through one night and the forenoon of the next day, only emerging into open water and clear weather off Cape Fraser.

TWO POLAR BEARS HARPOONED BY ESKIMOS
AND BROUGHT ABOARD AT BLACK LEAD, EAST GREENLAND

ARCTIC HUNTERS AND ESKIMOS
HAVING JUST LANDED THREE FINE SPECIMENS OF WALRUS

From this point we had a clear run through the middle of Robeson Channel, uninterrupted by either ice or fog, to Lady Franklin Bay. Here we encountered both ice and fog, and while working along in search of a practicable opening were forced across to the Greenland coast at Thank God Harbor. The fog lifted there, and enabled us to make out our whereabouts, and we steamed north through a series of leads past Cape Lupton, and thence southward toward Cape Union. A few miles off that cape we were stopped by impracticable ice, and we drifted back through to Cape Union, where we stopped again.

We lay for a time in a lake of water and then, to prevent being drifted south again we took refuge under the north shore of Lincoln Bay, in nearly the identical place where we had our unpleasant experiences three years before. Here we remained for several days during a period of constant and at times violent northeasterly winds.

Twice we were forced aground by the heavy ice; we had our port rail broken and a hole in the bulwark, and twice we pushed out in an attempt to get north, but we were forced back each time to our precarious shelter.

Finally on September 11 we squeezed around Cape Union and made fast in a shallow niche in the ice, but after some hours we made another short run to Black Cape, and hung on to a grounded bit of ice. At last, a little after midnight of September 5, we passed through extremely heavy running ice into a stream of open water, rounded Cape Union, and passed Cape Sheridan.

Within a quarter of an hour of the same time we arrived three years before, 7 a. m., September 5, we reached the open water extending beyond Cape Sheridan. We steamed up to the end of it, and it appeared practicable at first to reach Porter Bay, near Cape Joseph Henry, which I had for my winter quarters. But the outlook being unsatisfactory, I went back and put the *Roosevelt* into the only opening in the floe, being barred close to the mouth of the Sheridan River, a little north of our position three years ago.

The season was further advanced than in 1905, there was more snow on the ground, and the new ice inside the floe bergs was much thicker.

The work of discharging the ship was commenced at once, and rushed to completion. The supplies and equipment we sledded across ice and sea and deposited on shore. A house and workshop were built of board, covered with sails, and fitted with stoves, and the ship was snug for winter in shoal water, where she touched bottom at low tide. This settlement on the stormy shores of the Arctic Ocean was christened Hubbardville.

A hunting party was sent out on September 10, and a bear was brought in on the 12th, and some deer a day or two later.

On September 15 the full work of transporting supplies to Cape Columbia was commenced. Marvin, with Doctor Goodsell and Borup and the Eskimo, took sixteen sledges of supplies to Cape Belknap, and on the 25th the same party started with loads to Porter Bay. The work of hunting and transporting supplies was

prosecuted continuously by the members of the party and the Eskimos until November 5, when the supplies for the spring sledge trip had been removed from winter quarters and deposited at various places from Cape Colan to Cape Columbia.

In the latter part of September the movement of the ice subjected the ship to a pressure which listed her to port some 8 or 10 degrees, and she did not recover till the following spring.

On October 1 I went on a hunt with two Eskimos across the ice field and Parr Bay and the peninsula, made the circuit of Clements Markham Inlet, and returned to the ship in seven days with fifteen musk oxen, a bear, and a deer. Later in October I repeated the trip, obtaining five musk oxen, and hunting parties secured some forty deer.

Professor McMillan went to Columbia in November and obtained a month of tidal observations, returning in December. In the December moon Borup moved the Hecla depot to Cape Colan; Bartlett made a hunting trip overland to Lake Hazen, and Hensen went to Clements Markham Inlet. In the January moon Marvin crossed Robeson Channel and went to Cape Bryant for tidal and meteorological observations. Bartlett crossed the channel and made the circuit of Newman Bay and explored the peninsula. After he returned Goodsell went to Markham Inlet and Borup toward Lake Hazen, in the interior, on hunting trips.

In the February moon Bartlett went to Cape Hecla, Goodsell moved some more supplies from Hecla to Cape Colan, and Borup went to Markham Inlet on a hunting trip. On February 15 Bartlett left the *Roosevelt* with his division for Cape Columbia and Parr Bay; Goodsell, Borup, McMillan, and Hensen followed on successive days with their provisions. Marvin returned from Cape Bryant on February 17, and left for Cape Columbia February 21. I brought up in the rear February 22.

The total of all divisions leaving the *Roosevelt* were 7 members of the party, 59 Eskimos, 140 dogs, and 23 sledges. By February 27 such of the Cape Colan depot as was needed had been brought up to Cape Columbia, the dogs were rested and double-rationed and harnessed, and the sledges and other gear overhauled.

Four months of northerly winds during the fall and winter, instead of southerly ones, as during the previous season, led me to think that I would meet less water than before, but a great deal of rough ice, and I was prepared to hew a road through the jagged ice the first hundred miles or so, and then cross the big lead.

On the last day of February Bartlett, with his pioneer division, got away due north over the ice. On March 1 the remainder of the party got away on Bartlett's trail, and I followed an hour later.

The party now comprised 7 members of the expedition, 17 Eskimos, 133 dogs, and 19 sledges. One Eskimo and seven dogs had gone to pieces. A strong easterly wind, drifting snow, and temperature in the minus marked our departure from the camp at Cape Columbia, which I had christened Crane City.

SCENE ON SOUTH GREENLAND COAST,
SHOWING THE WAY THE ESKIMO WOMEN IN THIS LOCALITY DRESS THE HAIR

AN ARCTIC EXPLORER COMING OUT OF A SNOW COVERED IGLOO:
A WINTER HOME IN THE ARCTICS

Rough ice in the first march damaged several sledges and smashed two beyond repairs, the teams going to Columbia for other sledges in reserve there.

We camped ten miles from Crane City. The easterly wind and low temperature continued. On the 2d of March we passed the British record made by Markham, in May, 1876—82.20—and were stopped by open water, which had been formed by the wind after Bartlett passed. In this march we negotiated the lead, and reached Bartlett's third camp. Borup had gone back from here, but missed his way, owing to the faulting of the trail by the movement of the ice.

Marvin came back also for more fuel and alcohol. The wind continued, forming open water all about us. At the end of the fourth march we came upon Bartlett, who had been stopped by a wide lake of open water. We remained here from March 4 to March 11.

At noon of March 5, the sun, red and shaped like a football by excessed reflection, just raised itself above the horizon for a few minutes, and then disappeared again. It was the first time I had seen it since October 1.

I now began to feel a good deal of anxiety because there were no signs of Marvin and Borup, who should have been there for two days. Besides, they had the alcohol and oil which were indispensable for us. We concluded that they had either lost the trail or were imprisoned on an island by open water, probably the latter.

Fortunately, on March 11 the lead was practicable, and leaving a note for Marvin and Borup to push on after us by forced marches, we proceeded northward. The sounding of the lead gave 110 fathoms. During this march we crossed the 84th parallel, and traversed a succession of just frozen leads from a few hundred yards to a mile in width. This march was really simple.

On the 14th we got free of the leads and came on decent going. While we were making camp a courier from Marvin came, and informed me he was on the march in the rear. The temperature was 59 below zero.

The following morning, March 14, I sent Hensen with his division north to pioneer a trail for five marches, and Doctor Goodsell, according to the programme, started back to Cape Columbia. At night Marvin and Borup came spinning in with their men and dogs steaming in the bitter air like a squadron of battleships. Their arrival relieved me of all anxiety as to our oil supply.

In the morning I discovered that McMillan's foot was badly frost-bitten. The mishap had occurred two or three days before that, and McMillan had said nothing about it in the hope that it would come out all right. A glance at the injury showed me that the only thing was to send him back to Cape Columbia at once. The arrival of Marvin and Borup enabled me to spare sufficient men and dogs to go back with him.

This early loss of McMillan was seriously disappointing to me. He had a sledge all the way from Cape Columbia, and with his enthusiasm and the powers and physique of the trained athlete I had confidence in him for at least the 86th parallel, but there was no alternative.

The best sledges and dogs were selected and the sledge loads brought up to the standard. The sounding gave a depth of 325 fathoms. We were over the continental shelf, and, as I had surmised, the successive leads crossed in the fifth and sixth marches composed the big lead and marked the continental shelf.

On leaving this camp the expedition comprised 16 men, 12 sledges, and 100 dogs. The next march was satisfactory as regards distance and character of going. In the latter part there were pronounced movements in the ice, both visible and audible. Some leads were crossed, in one of which Borup and his team took a bath, and we were finally stopped by an impracticable lead opening in front of us.

We camped in a temperature of 50. At the end of two short marches we came upon Hensen and his party in camp mending their sledges. We devoted the remainder of the day to overhauling and mending sledges and breaking up our damaged ones for material.

The next morning I put Marvin in the lead to pioneer the trail, with instructions to make two forced marches to bring up our average, which had been cut down by the last two short ones. Marvin carried out his instructions implicitly. A considerable amount of young ice assisted in this.

At the end of the 10th of March, in latitude 85.23, Borup turned back in command of the second supporting party, having traveled a distance equivalent to Nansen's distance from this far to his farthest north. I was sorry to lose this young Yale runner, with his enthusiasm and pluck. He had led his heavy sledge over the floes in a way that commanded every one's admiration, and would have made his father's eyes glisten.

From this point the expedition comprised 12 men, 10 sledges, and 70 dogs. It was necessary for Marvin to take a sledge from here, and I put Bartlett and his division in advance to pioneer the trail.

The continual daylight enabled me to make a moderation here that brought my advance and main parties closer together, and reduced the likelihood of their being separated by open leads.

Bartlett left camp with Henderson and their division; Marvin and I remained with our divisions twenty hours longer, and then followed. When we reached Bartlett's camp, he broke out and went on, and we turned in. By this arrangement the advance party was traveling while the main party was asleep, and *vice versa*, and I was in touch with my advance party every twenty-four hours.

I had no reason to complain of the going for the next two marches, though for a less experienced party, less adaptable sledges, or less perfect equipment it would have been an impossibility.

At our position at the end of the second march Marvin obtained a satisfactory sight for latitude in clear weather, which placed us at 85.48. This result agreed very satisfactorily with the dead reckoning of Marvin, Bartlett, and myself.

Up to this time the slight altitude of the sun had made it not worth while to waste time in observations.

On the next two marches the going improved, and we covered good distances. In one of these marches a lead delayed us a few hours. We finally ferried across on the ice cakes.

The next day Bartlett let himself out, evidently for a record, and reeled off plump twenty miles. Here Marvin obtained another satisfactory sight on latitude which gave the position as 86.38 (or beyond the farthest north of Nansen and Abruzzi), and showed that we had covered 50 minutes of latitude in three marches. In these three marches we had passed the Norwegian record of 86.14 by Nansen and the Italian record of 86.34 by Cagni.

From this point Marvin turned back in command of the third supporting party. My last words to him were: "Be careful of the leads, my boy."

The party from this point comprised 9 men, 7 sledges, and 60 dogs. The conditions at this camp and the apparently unbroken expanse of fairly level ice in every direction reminded me of Cagni's description of his farthest north, but I was not deceived by the apparently favorable outlook, for favorable conditions never continue for any distance or any length of time in the Arctic regions.

The north march was very good going, but for the first time since leaving land we experienced that condition, frequent over these ice fields, of a hazy atmosphere in which the light is equal everywhere. All relief is destroyed, and it is impossible to see for any distance.

ESKIMOS ON THE ICE IN NORTH STAR BAY

We were obliged in this march to make a detour around an open lead. In the next march we encountered the heaviest and deepest snow of the journey through a thick, smothering mantle lying in the depressions of heavy rubble ice. I came upon Bartlett and his party, fagged out and temporarily discouraged by the heart-racking work of making a road.

I knew what was the matter with them. They were simply spoiled by the good going on the previous marches. I rallied them a bit, lightened their sledges, and set them on encouraged again.

During the next march we traveled through a thick haze, drifting over the ice before a biting air from the northeast. At the end of the march we came upon the captain camped beside a wide-open lead, with a dense black water sky northwest, north, and northeast. We built our igloos and turned in, but before I had fallen asleep I was roused out by a movement of the ice, and found a startling condition of affairs.

A rapidly widening road of black water ran but a few feet from our igloos. One of my teams of dogs had escaped by only a few feet from be-

SCENE AT ETAH, THE MOST NORTHERLY ESKIMO SETTLEMENT, SHOWING METHOD
OF DRYING MEAT, OUT OF THE REACH OF DOGS AND POLAR BEARS

ing dragged by the movement in the ice into the water.

Another team had an equally narrow escape from being crushed by the ice blocks piled over them. The ice on the north side of the lead was moving around eastward. The small floes on which were the captain's igloos were drifting eastward in the open water, and the side of our igloos threatened to follow suit.

Kicking out the door of the igloos, I called to the captain's men to pack their sledges and be ready for a quick dash when a favorable change arrived.

We hurried our things on our sledges, hitched the dogs, and moved on to a large floe west of us. Then leaving one man to look out for the dogs and sledges, we hurried over to assist the captain's party to join us.

A corner of their raft impinged on the ice on our side for the rest of the night, and during the next day the ice suffered the torments of the damned, surging together, opening out, groaning and grinding, while the open water belched black smoke like a prairie fire. Then the motion ceased, the open water closed, the atmosphere to the north was cleared, and we rushed across before the ice should open again.

A succession of literally open leads were crossed, and after them some heavy old ice, and then we came to a layer of young ice, some of which buckled under our sledges, and this gave us a straight way of six miles to the north. Then came more heavy old floes covered with hard snow. This was a good, long march.

The next march was a long one. It was Bartlett's last hit. He let himself out over a series of large old floes, steadily increasing in diameter and covered with hard snow.

During the last few miles I walked beside him or in advance. He was very solemn and anx-

ious to go further, but the programme was for him to go back from here in command of the fourth supporting party, and there were no supplies for an increase in the main party.

In this march we encountered a high wind for the first time since the three days after we left Cape Columbia. It was dead on our faces, bitter and insistent, but I had no reason to complain; it was better than an easterly or southerly wind, either of which would have set us adrift in open water, while this was closing up every lead behind. This furnished another advantage of my supporting parties. True, by so doing, it was pressing to the south the ice over which we traveled, and so robbing us of a hundred miles of advantage.

We concluded we were on or near the 88th parallel, unless the north wind had lost us several miles. The wind blew all night, and all the following day. At this camp in the morning Bartlett started to walk five or six miles to the north, to make sure of reaching the 88th parallel. While he was gone I selected the forty best dogs in the outfit and had them doubled, and I picked out five of the best sledges and assigned them expressly to the captain's party. I broke up the tent for material with which to repair the others and set Eskimos at this work.

Bartlett returned in time to take a satisfactory observation for latitude in clear weather, and obtained for our position 87.48, that showed that the continued north wind had robbed us of a number of miles of hard-earned distance. Bartlett took the observation here, as had Marvin five camps back, partly to save my eyes, but largely to give an independent record and determination of our advance. The observations completed, and two copies made, one for him and the other for me, Bartlett started on the back trail in command of my fourth supporting party, with 2 Eskimos, 1 sledge, and 18 dogs.

When he left I felt for a moment the pangs of regret as he disappeared in the distance, but it was only momentary. My work was still ahead, not in the rear. Bartlett had done good work, and had been a great help to me. Circumstances had thrust the brunt of pioneering upon him instead of dividing it among several, as I had planned.

He had reason to take pride in the fact that he had bettered the Italian record by a degree and a quarter, and had covered a distance equal to the entire distance of the Italian expedition from Franz Josef's Land to Cagni's farthest north. I had given Bartlett this position and post of honor in command of my fourth and last supporting party, and for two reasons: First, because of his magnificent handling of the *Roosevelt*; second, because he had cheerfully stood between me and many trifling annoyances on the expedition.

Then there was a third reason. It seemed to me appropriate, in view of the magnificent British record of Arctic work covering three centuries, that it should be a British subject who could boast that next to an American he had been nearest the pole.

With the disappearance of Bartlett, I turned to the problem before me. This was that for which I had worked for thirty-two years; for which I had lived the simple life; for which I had conserved all my energy on the upward trip; for which I had trained myself as for a race, crushing down every worry about success.

For success now, in spite of my years, I felt in trim—fit for the demands of the coming days and eager to be on the trail. As for my party, my equipment and my supplies, I was in shape beyond my most sanguine dreams of earliest

years. My party might be regarded as an ideal which had now come to realization—as loyal and responsive to my will as the fingers of my right hand.

Four of them carried the technique of dogs, sledges, ice, and cold as their heritage. Two of them, Hensen and Ootam, were my companions to the farthest point three years before. Two others, Egingwah and Sigloo, were in Clark's division, which had such a narrow escape at that time, and now were willing to go anywhere with my immediate party, and willing to risk themselves again in any supporting party.

The fifth was a young man who had never served before in any expedition, but who was, if possible, even more willing and eager than the others for the princely gifts—a boat, a rifle, a shotgun, ammunition, knives, etc.—which I had promised to each of them who reached the pole with me: for he knew that these riches would enable him to wrest from a stubborn father the girl whose image filled his hot young heart.

All had blind confidence so long as I was with them and gave no thought for the morrow, sure that whatever happened I should somehow get them back to land. But I dealt with the party equally. I recognized that all its impetus centered in me and that, whatever pace I set, it would make good. If any one was played out, I would stop for a short time.

I had no fault to find with the conditions. My dogs were the very best, the pick of 122 with which we left Columbia. Almost all were powerful males, hard as nails, in good flesh, but without a superfluous ounce, without a suspicion of fat anywhere; and, what was better yet, they were all in good spirits.

My sledges, now that the repairs were completed, were in good condition. My supplies

AN ESKIMO, HIS WIFE, SONS, AND DAUGHTERS

AN ESKIMO MOTHER AND BABE

were ample for forty days, and with the reserve, represented by the dogs themselves, could be made to last fifty.

Pacing back and forth in the lee of the pressure ridge where our igloos were built, while my men got their loads ready for the next marches, I settled on my programme. I decided that I should strain every nerve to make five marches of twenty-five miles each, crowding these marches in such a way as to bring up to the end of the fifth long enough before noon to permit the immediate taking of an observation for latitude.

Weather and leads permitting, I believed I could do this. If my proposed distances were cut down by any chance, I had two means in reserve for making up the deficit.

First. To make the last march a forced one, stopping to make tea and rest the dogs, but not to sleep.

Second. At the end of the fifth march to make a forced march with a light sledge, a double team of dogs, and one or two of the party, leaving the rest in camp.

Underlying all these calculations was a recognition of the ever-present neighborhood of open leads and impassable water, and the knowledge that a twenty-four hour gale would knock all my plans into a cocked hat, and even put us in imminent peril.

At a little after midnight of April 1, after a few hours of sound sleep, I hit the trail, leaving the others to break up camp and follow. As I climbed the pressure ridge back of our igloos, I set another hole in my belt, the third since I started. Every man and dog of us was lean and flat-bellied as a board, and as hard.

It was a fine morning. The wind of the last two days had subsided, and the going was the best and most equable of any I had yet. The floes were large and old, hard and clear, and were surrounded by pressure ridges, some of which were almost stupendous. The biggest of them, however, were easily negotiated, either through some crevice or up some huge brink.

I set a good pace for about ten hours. Twenty-five miles took me well beyond the 88th parallel. While I was building my igloos a long lead formed by the east and southeast of us at a distance of a few miles.

A few hours' sleep and we were on the trail again. As the going was now practically horizontal, we were unhampered and could travel as long as we pleased and sleep as little as we wished. The weather was fine and the going like that of the previous day, except at the beginning, when pickaxes were required. This and a brief stop at another lead cut down our distance. But we had made twenty miles in ten hours and were half way to the 89th parallel.

The ice was grinding audibly in every direction, but no motion was visible. Evidently it was settling back in equilibrium and probably sagging due northward with its release from the wind pressure.

Again there was a few hours' sleep, and we hit the trail before midnight. The weather and going were even better. The surface, except as interrupted by infrequent ridges, was as level as the glacial fringe from Hecla to Columbia and harder.

We marched something over ten hours, the dogs being often on the trot and made 20 miles. Near the end of the march, we rushed across a lead 100 yards wide, which buckled under our sledges, and finally broke as the last sledge left it.

We stopped in sight of the 89th parallel, in a temperature of 40 degrees below. Again a scant sleep, and we were on our way once more and across the 89th parallel.

This march duplicated the previous one as to weather and going. The last few hours it was on young ice, and occasionally the dogs were galloping. We made 25 miles or more, the air, the sky, and the bitter wind burning the face till it cracked. It was like the great interior ice cap of Greenland. Even the natives complained of the bitter air. It was as keen as frozen steel.

A little longer sleep than the previous ones had to be taken here as we were all in need of it. Then on again.

Up to this time, with each successive march, our fears of an impossible lead had increased. At every inequality of the ice, I found myself hurrying breathlessly forward, fearing that it marked a lead, and when I arrived at the summit would catch my breath with relief— only to find myself hurrying on in the same way at the next one. But on this march, by some strange shift and feeling, this fear fell from me completely. The weather was thick, but it gave me no uneasiness.

Before I turned in I took an observation, which indicated our position as 89.25. A dense, lifeless pall hung overhead. The horizon was black and the ice beneath was a ghastly, shelly-white, with no relief—a striking contrast to the glimmering, sunlit fields of it over which we had been traveling for the previous four days.

The going was even better and there was scarcely any snow on the hard, granular, last summer's surface of the old floes dotted with the sapphire ice of the previous summer's lakes.

A rise in temperature to 15 below reduced the friction of the sledges and gave the dogs the appearance of having caught the spirit of the party. The more sprightly ones, as they went along with tightly-curled tails, frequently tossed their heads, with short, sharp barks and yelps.

In twelve hours we made 40 miles. There was not a sign of a lead in the march.

I had now made my five marches, and was in time for a hasty noon observation through a temporary break in the clouds, which indicated our position as 89.57. I quote an entry from my journal some hours later:

"The pole at last! The prize of three centuries. My dream and goal for twenty years! Mine at last! I cannot bring myself to realize it. It all seems so simple and commonplace. As Bartlett said when turning back, when speaking of his being in these exclusive regions which no mortal has ever penetrated before, 'It's just like every day.'"

Of course I had my sensations that made sleep impossible for hours, despite my utter fatigue—the sensations of a lifetime; but I have no room for them here.

The first thirty hours at the pole were spent in taking observations; in going some ten miles beyond our camp, and some eight miles to the right of it; in taking photographs, planting my flags, depositing my records, studying the horizon with my telescope for possible land, and searching for a practicable place to make a sounding.

Ten hours after our arrival, the clouds cleared before a slight breeze from our left, and from that time until our departure in the afternoon of April 7, the weather was cloudless and flawless. The minimum temperature during the thirty hours was 33 below, the maximum 12.

We had reached the goal, but the return was still before us. It was essential that we reach the land before the next spring tide, and we must strain every nerve to do this.

CHILDREN OF THE TOP OF THE WORLD

I had a brief talk with my men. From now on, it was to be a big travel, little sleep, and a hustle every minute. We would try, I told them, to double march on the return—that is, to start and cover one of our northward marches, make tea and eat our luncheon in the igloos, then cover another march, eat and sleep a few hours, and repeat this daily.

As a matter of fact, we nearly did this, covering regularly on our return journey five outward marches in three return marches. Just as long as we could hold the trail we could double our speed, and we need waste no time in building new igloos.

Every day that we gained on the return lessened the chances of a gale destroying the track. Just above the 87th parallel was a region fifty miles wide, which caused me considerable uneasiness. Twelve hours of strong easterly, westerly or northerly wind would make this region an open sea.

In the afternoon of the 7th we started on our return, having double-fed the dogs, repaired the sledges for the last time, and discarded all our spare clothing to lighten the loads.

Five miles from the pole a narrow crack filled with recent ice, through which we were able to work a hole with a pick-axe, enabled me to make a sounding. All my wire, 1,500 fathoms, was sent down, but there was no bottom. In pulling up the wire parted a few fathoms from the surface, and lead and wire went to the bottom. Off went the reel and handle, lightening the sledges still further. We had no more use for them now.

Three marches brought us back to the igloos where the Captain turned back. The last march was in the wild sweep of a northerly gale, with drifting snow and the ice rocking under us as we dashed over it.

South of where Marvin had turned back we came to where his party had built several igloos while delayed by open leads. Still further south we found where the Captain bad been held up by an open lead and obliged to camp. Fortunately, the movement of these leads was simply open and shut, and it took considerable water motion to fault the trail seriously.

While the Captain and Marvin, as was found out later, and Borup had been delayed by open leads, we seemed to bear a patent charm and at no single lead were we delayed more than a couple of hours. Sometimes the ice was fast and firm enough to carry us across; sometimes a short detour, sometimes a brief halt for the lead to close, sometimes an improvised ferry on an ice-cake, kept the trail without difficulty down to the tenth outward march.

Igloos there disappeared completely, and the entire region was unrecognizable. Where on the outward journey had been narrow cracks, there were now broad leads, one of them over five miles in width, caught over with young ice.

Here again fortune favored us, and no pronounced movement of the ice having taken place since the Captain passed we had his trail to follow. We picked up the old trail again north of the seventh igloos, followed it beyond the fifth, and at the big lead lost it finally.

From here we followed the Captain's trail, and on April 23 our sledges passed up the vertical edge of the glacier fringe, a little west of Cape Columbia. When the last sledge came up I thought my Eskimos had gone crazy. They yelled and called and danced themselves helpless. As Ooath sat down on his sledge he remarked in Eskimo:

"The Devil is asleep or having trouble with his wife, or we never should have come back so easily."

A STRIKING SCENE IN THE ARCTIC REGIONS: EXPLORERS' SHIPS, ICE BERGS,
AND ICE FLOATS: VERY GOOD WHALE FISHING IS TO BE FOUND HERE, BAFFIN BAY

A few hours later we arrived at Crane City under the bluffs of Cape Columbia, and after putting four pounds of pemmican into each of the faithful dogs to keep them quit, we had at last our chance to sleep. Never shall I forget that sleep at Cape Columbia. It was sleep, sleep, then turn over and sleep again. We slept gloriously, with never a thought of the morrow or of having to walk, and, too, with no thought that there was to be never a night more of blinding headache. Cold water to a parched throat is nothing compared with sleep to a numbed, fatigued brain and body.

Two days we spent here in sleeping and drying our clothes; then for the ship. Our dogs, like ourselves, had not been hungry when we arrived, but simply lifeless with fatigue. They were different animals, and the better ones among them stept on with tightly curled tails, uplifted heads, and their hind legs treading the snow with piston-like regularity. We reached Hecla in one march, and the *Roosevelt* in another.

When we got to the *Roosevelt*, I was staggered by the news of the fatal mishap to Marvin. He had either been less cautious or less fortunate than the rest of us, and his death emphasized the risk to which we had all been subjected, for there was not one of us but had been in the sledge during some time in the journey.

The big lead, cheated of its prey three years before, had at last gained its human victim.

The rest can be quickly told. McMillan and Borup had started for the Greenland coast to deposit caches for me. Before I arrived a flying Eskimo courier from me overtook them with instructions that the caches were no longer needed, and that they were to concentrate their energies on tidal observations, etc., at Cape Morris Jesup, and north from there.

These instructions were carried out, and after their return in latter part of May, McMillan made some further tidal observations at other points. The supplies remaining at the various caches were brought in, and on July 18 the *Roosevelt* left her winter quarters and was driven out into the channel pack of Cape Nion.

She fought her way south in the center of the channel, and passed Cape Sabine on August 8, or thirty-nine days earlier than in 1908, and thirty-two days earlier than the British expedition in 1876.

We picked up Whitney and his party and the stores at Etah. We killed 70 odd walrus for my Eskimos, whom I landed at their homes. We met the *Jeanie* off Saunders Island and took over her coal, and cleared from Cape York on August 26, one month earlier than in 1906.

On September 5 we arrived at Indian Harbor, whence the message, "Stars and Stripes nailed to North Pole," was sent vibrating southward through the crisp Labrador air.

The culmination of long experience, a thorough knowledge of the conditions of the problem, gained in the last expedition—these together with new sledges, which reduced the work of both dogs and driver, and a new type of camp cooker, which added to the comfort and increased the hours of sleep of the men's party, combined to make the present expedition an agreeable improvement on the last in respect to the rapidity and effectiveness of its work, and the lessened discomfort and strain upon the members of the party.

As to the personnel, I have again been particularly fortunate. Captain Bartlett is just Bartlett—tireless, sleepless, enthusiastic, whether on the bridge, or in the crow's nest, or at the head of a sledge division in the field.

Dr. Goodsell, the surgeon of the expedition, not only looked after its health and his own specialty of microscopes, but took his full share of the field work of the expedition as well, and was always ready for any work.

Profs. Marvin and McMillan have secured a mass of scientific data, having made all the tidal and most of the field work, and their services were invaluable in every way.

Borup not only made the record as to the distance traveled during the journey, but to his assistance and expert knowledge of photography is due what I believe to be the unequalled series of photographs taken by the expedition.

Henson in the field and Percy as steward, were the same as ever, invaluable in their respective lines. Chief Engineer Wardwell, also of the last expedition, aided by his assistant,

Scott, kept the machinery up to a high state of efficiency and has given the *Roosevelt* the force and power which enabled her to negotiate apparently impracticable ice.

Mr. Gushue, the mate, who was in charge of the *Roosevelt* during the absence of Captain Bartlett and myself, and Boatswain Murphy, who was put in charge of the station at Etah for the relief of Cook, were both trustworthy and reliable men, and I count myself fortunate in having had them in my service.

The members of the crew and the firemen were a distinct improvement over those of the last expedition. Every one of them was willing and anxious to be of service in every possible way. Connors, who was promoted to be boatswain in the absence of Murphy, proved to be particularly effective. Barnes, seaman, and Wise-

SCENE ON THE GREENLAND COAST

man and Joyce. firemen, not only assisted Marvin and McMillan in their tidal meteorological observations on the *Roosevelt*, but Wiseman and Barnes went into the field with them on their trips to Cape Columbia, and Condon and Cody covered 1,000 miles hunting and sledging supplies.

As for my faithful Eskimos, I have left them with ample supplies of dark, rich walrus meat and blubber for their winter, with currants, sugar, biscuits, guns, rifles, ammunition, knives, hatchets, traps, etc., and for the splendid four who stood beside me at the pole a boat and tent each to requite them for their energy, and the hardships and toil they underwent to help their friend Peary to the North Pole.

But all of this—the dearly bought years of experience, the magnificent strength of the *Roosevelt*, the splendid energy and enthusiasm of my party, the loyal faithfulness of my Eskimos—would have gone for naught but for the faithful necessaries of war furnished so loyally by the members of the Peary Arctic Club. And it is no detraction from the living to say that to no single individual has the fine result been more signally due than to my friend the late Morris K. Jesup, the first President of the Club.

Their assistance has enabled me to tell the last of the great earth stories, the story the world has been waiting to hear for 300 years—the story of the discovery of the North Pole.

THE NORTH POLE

AT a meeting of the Board of Managers of the National Geographic Society, Wednesday morning, October 20, the records and observations and proof of Commander Robert E. Peary that he reached the pole April 6, 1909, were submitted to the Society. The only question now to be decided by the association is whether or not Commander Peary reached the pole on this date, as claimed.

The records and observations were immediately referred to the Committee on Research, with the direction that the Chairman appoint a sub-committee of experts, of which he shall be a member, to examine said records and report on them to the Board. Mr. Henry Gannett, Chairman of the Committee on Research, immediately appointed as the other members of the Committee Rear Admiral Colby M. Chester, U. S. Navy, and O. H. Tittmann, Superintendent of the U. S. Coast and Geodetic Survey.

This Committee of the Society will personally examine the note-books and original observations made by Commander Peary in his march to the pole, and see all the papers as brought back from the field. The Committee will report to the Board the result of its findings at a special meeting of the Board to be called for that purpose.

This action of the Society was taken in accordance with the by-laws of the Society, which provide that "The Committee on Research shall be charged with the consideration of all matters of scientific and technical geography, including exploration, which may be brought before the Society, or which may originate in the Committee; and shall report thereon to the Board of Managers, with recommendations for action."

At a meeting on October 1, the Board of Managers stated that the National Geographic Society could accept the personal statements of neither Commander Peary nor Dr. Cook that the pole had been reached, without investigation by its Committee on Research or by a scientific body acceptable to it.

At the same meeting Commander Peary and Dr. Cook were urged speedily to submit their observations to a competent scientific commission in the United States.

At a later meeting the Board joined in a request from the American Museum of Natural History, New York, and the American Geographical Society to President Ira Remsen that he, as the President of the National Academy of Sciences, appoint a commission to pass upon the records of Commander Peary and Dr. Cook. This plan for an early examination failed, as Dr. Remsen stated that he would not be able to appoint said commission unless authorized by his Council, which meets late in November, and unless also requested to do so by both Commander Peary and Dr. Cook.

Commander Peary was willing to abide by such a commission, but Dr. Cook stated that his observations would go first to the University of Copenhagen. In view of the fact that Commander Peary had been waiting since his return to submit his records to a scientific commission in the United States, the National Geographic Society believed it should receive his papers now in order that his claim of having reached the pole may be passed upon without further delay.

The Society is ready to make a similar examination of Dr. Cook's original observations and field notes, but as he promised to send them to the University of Copenhagen, and the Society will not have an opportunity of seeing them for probably some months, it did not seem fair to defer action on Commander Peary's observations until Dr. Cook's papers were received by the Society. The only question now to be decided by the Society is whether or not Commander Peary reached the pole on April 6, 1909.

The following cablegram has been received by the Society from the University of Copenhagen, in reply to the Society's request that the University of Copenhagen waive its first claim to Dr. Cook's records, in order that the records might be immediately examined in the United States and considerable delay avoided:

"October 20, 1909.
National Geographic Society,
      Washington.
    University regrets not able comply with your request.

Torp, *Rektor*."

Mr. Henry Gannett, Chairman of the Committee which will report on Commander Peary's observations, has been Chief Geographer of the U. S. Geological Survey since 1882; he is the author of "Manual of Topographic Surveying," "Statistical Atlases of the Tenth and Eleventh Censuses," "Dictionary of Altitudes," "Magnetic Declination in the United States," Stanford's "Compendium of Geography," and of many government reports. Mr. Gannett is Vice-President of the National Geographic Society, and was one of the founders of the Society in 1888.

Rear Admiral Colby M. Chester, U. S. Navy, was graduated from the U. S. Naval Academy in 1863. He has held practically every important command under the Navy Department, including Superintendent of the U. S. Naval Observatory, Commander-in-Chief Atlantic Squadron, Superintendent of the U. S. Naval Academy, Chief of Hydrographic Division, U. S. Navy. Admiral Chester has been known for many years as one of the best and most particular navigators in the service.

O. H. Tittmann has been Superintendent of the U. S. Coast and Geodetic Survey since 1900. He is the member for the United States of the Alaskan Boundary Commission, and was one of the founders of the National Geographic Society.

THE NORTH POLE

THE Board of Managers of the National Geographic Society, at a meeting held at Hubbard Memorial Hall November 4, 1909, received the following report:

The sub-committee to which was referred the task of examining the records of Commander Peary in evidence of his having reached the North Pole, beg to report that they have completed their task.

Commander Peary has submitted to this sub-committee his original journal and records of observations, together with all his instruments and apparatus, and certain of the most important of the scientific results of his expedition. These have been carefully examined by your sub-committee, and they are unanimously of the opinion that Commander Peary reached the North Pole on April 6, 1909.

They also feel warranted in stating that the organization, planning, and management of the expedition, its complete success, and its scientific results, reflect the greatest credit on the ability of Commander Robert E. Peary, and render him worthy of the highest honors that the National Geographic Society can bestow upon him.

HENRY GANNETT.
C. M. CHESTER.
O. H. TITTMANN.

The foregoing report was unanimously approved.

Immediately after this action the following resolutions were unanimously adopted:

WHEREAS, Commander Robert E. Peary has reached the North Pole, the goal sought for centuries,

WHEREAS, This is the greatest geographical achievement that this Society can have opportunity to honor, therefore

Resolved, That a special medal be awarded to Commander Peary.

Resolved, That the question of whether or not any one reached the North Pole prior to 1909 be referred to the Committee on Research with instructions to recommend to the Board of Managers a sub-committee of experts who shall have authority to send for papers or make such journeys as may be necessary to inspect original records, and that this action of the Society be communicated at once to those who may have evidence of importance.

Resolved, That in view of the able seamanship, pertinacious effort, and able management of Captain C. A. Bartlett, displayed during the Peary Arctic Expedition of 1908–1909, and that he reached the high latitude of 87° 40′ north, he be awarded a medal by the National Geographic Society.

At a meeting of the Board of Managers November 8, the Committee on Research of the Society recommended that the personnel of the committee to consider whether the pole was discovered before 1909 should be entirely different from that of the committee which passed on the Peary records. Upon their recommendation the Board appointed the following committee:

J. Howard Gore, formerly Professor of Mathematics, George Washington University, and author of several works on surveying and geodesy.

Rear Admiral John E. Pillsbury, U. S. N., who was for ten years in charge of the hydro-graphic office of the U. S. Navy, did important work investigating the gulf stream currents, was for several years Assistant Chief of the Bureau of Navigation of the Navy Department, and later Chief of Staff of the North Atlantic Squadron.

Dr. C. Willard Hayes, Chief Geologist of the U. S. Geological Survey, one of the pioneer explorers of Alaska and of many sections of the Rocky Mountains.

Vol. XXI, No. 1   WASHINGTON   January, 1910

THE DISCOVERY OF THE NORTH POLE

THE principal feature of the Annual Banquet of the National Geographic Society, December 15th, was the presentation of a special gold medal to Commander Robert E. Peary, United States Navy, for the discovery of the pole, and of Hubbard medals to Captain Robert Bartlett for attaining the farthest north, and to Grove Karl Gilbert for achievements in physiographic research. Telegrams of congratulation were read during the evening from former President Theodore Roosevelt, who, on behalf of the Society, presented the Hubbard medal of the National Geographic Society to Commander Robert E. Peary in 1906; from the Duke of the Abruzzi, and from the Geographical Society of London and the Geographical Society of Berlin.

About five hundred members and guests attended the banquet, including representatives from many foreign countries and from all parts of the United States. Toasts were responded to by the Dean of the Diplomatic Corps, the Italian Ambassador, Baron Mayor des Planches; the French Ambassador, Hon. J. J. Jusserand; the British Ambassador, Hon. James Bryce; Speaker Cannon, Andrew Carnegie, Admiral Colby M. Chester, Professor J. Howard Gore, General Thomas Hubbard, President of the Peary Arctic Club, and Hon. John Barrett.

The medals have been inscribed as follows:

A Special Medal Awarded by the National Geographic Society to Robert E. Peary for the Discovery of the North Pole, April 6, 1909.

The Hubbard Medal Awarded by the National Geographic Society to Robert A. Bartlett, Commander of the S. S. *Roosevelt*, for attaining the Farthest North, 87° 48', March 31, 1909.

The Hubbard Medal Awarded by the National Geographic Society to Grove Karl Gilbert for original investigations and achievements in Physiographic Research during a period of thirty years.

The telegrams received were as follows:

Nairobi, *December* 12, 1909.
National Geographic Society, Washington:
Extremely pleased. Desire through you to extend heartiest congratulations Peary on his great feat which you have thus recognized.
Roosevelt.

LONDON, *December* 15, 1909.
National Geographic Society, Washington:
Hearty congratulations to Peary on medal. Highly gratified at medal to Bartlett.

DARWIN,
President, Royal Geographical Society.

BERLIN, *December* 15.
COMMANDER PEARY,
National Geographic Society, Washington:
The Geographical Society of Berlin sends to its honorary member heartiest congratulations on these honors well deserved because of your conquest of the pole which is rich in results, and hopes early in the spring to be able to similarly honor you here.

WAHNSCHAFFE, President.

THE TOASTMASTER, WILLIS L. MOORE, PRESIDENT NATIONAL GEOGRAPHIC SOCIETY

On behalf of the Board of Managers of the National Geographic Society and of the fifty thousand and over members of the organization, and especially of the three hundred and fifty members of the Society gathered at these tables tonight, I extend to you, our guests, a hearty greeting. We are met to celebrate a great achievement. This is an Arctic night at the pole. But we trust that the fervor of our greeting for you will be tropical in its significance.

And with that word of greeting to you we will begin the exercises of the evening, and we shall endeavor to dismiss the gathering within a reasonable time. That is a little intimation that we do not expect very long speeches from any particular individual. I will make exceptions to that on the part of the three Ambassadors on my right and left. They cannot talk too long for the National Geographic Society. One comes to us from that nation that has given so much to the world in literature and art, the mellowing influence of its beauty and antiquity shedding a soft refulgence throughout the entire world. A member of the royal family of that nation was entertained in this very room three or four years ago, who has achieved great honor in Arctic exploration, and we have a word from him tonight. I shall introduce the Ambassador from Italy, Baron Mayor des Planches, to say a few words and give us that message. The Ambassador from Italy.

THE ITALIAN AMBASSADOR— BARON MAYOR DES PLANCHES

Mr. President, ladies and gentlemen: I remember having been present at another banquet given by the National Geographic Society, in which Commander Peary was, as he is now, the guest of honor.

Commander Peary had already at that time reached the highest polar latitude, beating the record of a young Italian explorer, the Duke of the Abruzzi. I had not, then, special instructions to congratulate the Commander for the splendid result he had already obtained, but I was sure that His Royal Highness, chivalrous as he always is, was applauding the achievement of his fortunate rival. I expressed to the winner the felicitations of the defeated, and the Duke afterwards cordially approved of what I had done.

Now things are different. As soon as I received the kind invitation of your President to be here tonight, I cabled to the Duke that I would have the pleasure of meeting the glorious conqueror of the pole. A few hours after I received the cablegram which I ask your permission to translate:

"Many thanks to you for giving me the opportunity to express to Commander Peary my heartfelt felicitations. Tell him in my behalf that I am happy that the pole has been discovered by the explorer whose courage and perseverance deserved such a reward.

LOUIS OF SAVOIA."

THE FRENCH AMBASSADOR— HON. J. J. JUSSERAND

Mr. President, ladies and gentlemen: Two years ago we were gathered together, almost day for day, in this same room, under the same chairman who has just spoken in such touching words of my country, and such undeserved ones of her representative; and we were gathered together also to commemorate a pole discovery. It was the discovery of the magnetic pole. I was asked to say a few words. Offering to you excuses for quoting myself, I beg permission to recall that, considering the time to come, I expressed myself thus: "Some new expedition, led through air or through water, by some maybe among the men present here today, will certainly, in the near future, gain the first sight of the long-sought North Pole." And looking at the list of those present on that day, I find that there appeared the name of "Commander and Mrs. Robert E. Peary." I think I may say that, once in my life, I spoke as a prophet.

Momentous changes have come to pass in the world and in this land. For a very long time, during the period to which our chairman alluded just now, America was not the land that produced explorers, but the land for explorers to seek. The day in August, 1492, when a certain Spanish ship left Palos and floated across the unknown sea, resulted in the revelation to wondering nations of a new, unsuspected, and immense world; and the energies of all those who wanted to discover, to learn, to win, to explore, to get fame and wealth for themselves and their country, were bent for centuries toward this continent more than toward any other part of the globe. The ocean was crossed and recrossed by the tiny crafts of some of the best sons of France, England, Italy, Holland, Spain, Portugal, Scandinavia. We French certainly did our part, as we explored further inland than any, and made known to the world the resources and beauty of the valley watered by the "Mechacébé."

For a very long time, indeed, it was the desire of the pluckiest to come to these shores and explore those new regions so extraordinary, so beautiful, yet so thoroughly unknown that it took till our own lifetime to get a somewhat accurate idea of their contents. Many of us were already in our manhood when the Yellowstone Park was revealed to the admiration of the world.

But before that moment a great change had taken place; the field for exploration bad begun to produce explorers, and it has never ceased since; explorers of unknown lands, like Rockhill, Crosby, and many others; explorers of the depth of the seas, like Agassiz; of the realms of electricity, like Graham Bell and Edison; of the sun, like Doctor Hale; of ancient Babylonic civilizations, like those scientific missionaries sent abroad by the Chicago University, and explorers, above all, of that unknown world into which French Montgolfier was the first to rise, the world of air, mastered by the plucky men of our day, in the front rank of whom stand your famous compatriots, the brothers Wright.

And while so many explorations went on, one remained ceaselessly striven for, ceaselessly unachieved: the one that had for its object the conquest of the pole. The longing for that discovery is of a comparatively recent date, but once its hold on mankind began, it proved one of the most ardent men had yet experienced.

The ancients had not evinced any great anxiety about the polar regions. They knew the north was a strange frozen place with weird legends about it, a region, said Tacitus, where looking toward the east one can see Phoebus rise: "The sound he makes on emerging from the waters can be heard, and the form of his steeds is visible."

In the last century, the problem became for mankind one of intense interest, one which *had* to be solved, were it, as indeed it was, at the cost of many an heroic life. And the great labor began, never to be interrupted until could be possible such a gathering as today's, in which the National Geographic Society of America is to bestow its medal on the now most famous of its members. Long was the search and hard was the toil, from the days of Sir John Franklin and Kane to those of Nansen, Nordenskiold, royal Abruzzi, and your admirable Greely remaining three years unrevictualed in the frozen north.

I well remember how, in days long past, I followed as a child, with my brother and sisters, our hearts beating with emotion, the efforts of one of the imaginary heroes of that prophet-novelist, Jules Verne; a prophet-novelist indeed, for most of what he fancied has become reality; his fancy submarines have become our real ones, the world he announced where everything would be done by electricity is now near at hand; his dream dirigibles have become our tangible ones, and the conquest of the pole, which he foresaw, is now a fact. He described it in advance, and not so badly, for he told us that, at the pole, there was no land, but only sea, and Commander Peary has just returned to tell us that it is so. Truth to say, the writer asserted that the sea was an open one, and I have present in my mind, as if it were a thing of yesterday, a view of that open sea pictured in his book, and along its shore quantity of birds, the like of which, I am afraid, Commander Peary had not the satisfaction of killing and eating. But as you know, there is no prophet so good that does not make now and then some little mistake.

Well, after that long search, and so many proofs of endurance and valor given by many, the deed is done and the coveted prize belongs to you, Americans. If we, French, did not do much for the solution of the problem, busy as we were, and usefully busy, exploring elsewhere in Asia, Africa, South America, we know full well what peerless merit there was in doing what your compatriot has accomplished, and about which what there is to say is going to be expressed by our learned chairman tonight. Commander Peary will allow me to offer him a tribute of admiration, and the congratulations of my country for the fame he has won and the deed he has accomplished.

THE TOASTMASTER

We have at our tables many representatives from our National Congress from both houses of that great body. We mean no disparagement to the legislative institutions of any other country when I say that the American people have a proper reverence and respect for their own representatives. I do not believe that there is a cleaner, an abler body of national representatives met anywhere in the world than the National Legislature of the United States. We are honored tonight by having at our board the Speaker of the House of Representatives. People do not apply an endearing term to a public man that they do not down deep in their hearts respect, and I shall, as an honor to the National Geographic Society, ask the Speaker of the National House of Representatives to say a word at this board.

SPEAKER CANNON

Mr. President, ladies and gentlemen of the National Geographic Society, and guests: It is supposed that the present incumbent of the Speaker's chair is a czar. Such being the case, the rules of the House in committee of the whole on the state of the Union will be enforced; that is, the five-minute rule. Note the time and let your gavel fall at the end of five minutes, unless I leave the floor earlier than that.

I am glad to be here. I am glad that the National Geographic Society have settled one thing. Peary or Cook found the North Pole, and you stated which, and I have implicit confidence in your judgment. How marvelously the nineteenth century has witnessed the opening of events which three hundred years prior thereto the nations of Europe sent in their colonies to the new continent to struggle for mastery. Their bones are dust and their souls are with the saints, but the coming of the French and the German and the Scandinavian and the inhabitants of Great Britain, and the present coming of the Italians and the Hungarians, and the Spanish who came first and wrought great things in the new continent, have settled all questions. We are glad to congratulate ourselves in the United States that we have the most enterprising and of the best of those countries that have made our own country their country, and have been assimilated and form our civilization. You cannot sing the *Banzai* national air, you cannot sing "The Campbells Are Coming," you cannot sing "The Watch on the Rhine"—which always seemed to me in comparison with all the other music like the grind-

ing of a great glacier—you cannot sing them anywhere in the boundaries of the Republic but what the huzzas will come. How marvelously the progress!

I am but yet a young man, and yet I recollect very well when it was gravely proposed in the Senate of the United States that a statue should be erected to the god Terminus on the peaks of the Rocky Mountains, and that should be our western boundary. All questions of territory have been settled, and the United States is the common territory of what we can gladly say is the best blood of the European countries. I say best blood because the enterprising young men come to new countries that promise in their judgment a reward for their enterprise and courage. I am glad that the North Pole has been found. I am glad for many reasons. In the first place it will stop adventurers after notoriety or adventurers in fact from endeavoring to discover the pole. We know now whether there is land there, and I am glad to know there is no land there and I can prove it by Peary, because there is no chance for any discussion about the conservation of natural resources. There can be no ice factory, because it is brackish and the ice would be worthless.

I am glad to be with this Society. I have had many invitations. It has so happened that this is the first one that I have been able to accept. But, after looking into your faces and congratulating you over the history of this Society—over the founder of the Society, who has crossed over, but his work is still with us—and after congratulating Commander Peary, I pay my respects to the representatives of the many great governments here tonight and will just in one sentence sit down. When next, Mr. President, John Gilpin rides, may I be there to see.

THE TOASTMASTER

Many of our guests are familiar with the aims and objects of the National Geographic Society; all are not, and so I shall introduce for a few minutes our Professor J. Howard Gore, Professor Emeritus of George Washington University, a member of the Board of Managers, to tell you something of the aims and objects of this institution.

THE NATIONAL GEOGRAPHIC SOCIETY—BY JAMES HOWARD GORE

In some future edition of the Book of Proverbs it may be written: "Whoso tooteth not his own horn, yea verily the horn of the same may not be tooted." The President of this Society must have anticipated the wisdom of this injunction when he asked me to be the horn soloist for the Society.

To our colleague, Mr. Henry Gannett, is given the credit of having originated the flattering invitation, "Sit down five minutes and tell me all you know." If this idea was in the mind of our President when he asked me to tell all I knew of the activities of the National Geographic Society in ten minutes I hope he intends that I shall keep the change, for it will not need so much time to traverse in outline this topic, though its bounds be the points in which the ultimate east meets the ultimate west and the north has the south for its antipode.

That we exist is attested by a membership of more than 50,000, and the question as to why we exist must be answered favorably by the thousands who each year come into our ranks.

I was greatly impressed a few years ago by a set of drawings showing the way in which geography is taught in the public schools of Brussels. The first of the series showed the plan of the classroom, with the position of the pupil's desk. The second gave the floor-plan of the building with special indication to mark the room which was the entirety of the first lesson. As lesson followed lesson the pupil had located the building with respect to the prominent buildings of the city, the situation of the city with respect to the other cities of the kingdom, the outlines of the kingdom, the place of the same in the continent of Europe, Europe's place on the eastern hemisphere, and finally a map of the entire world.

In this way the pupil oriented himself with respect to his playmates and their immediate surroundings with respect to the great world of which they were parts. But in the lessening scale the pupil, though great in his own conceit, dwindled as lesson followed lesson and the world of which he formed a part grew vastly in importance.

The proper study of mankind is man—not man in his littleness, in his finiteness, but the house in which he lives, the town in which he dwells, the land he calls home, and the world over which he roams. Each day's walk takes him to a different point and every day's journey gives to him a new geographic position.

The air he breathes is wafted along by purifying currents whose movements we strive to know. The water that slakes his thirst follows courses whose meanderings we want to trace; the paths he treads, the roads he travels and the oceans on which he journeys must find places upon our charts.

The purpose of our Society is to know these things and to diffuse abroad our knowledge. We seek new facts through exploration and we scatter them over the civilized world on the pages of the best geographic magazine that finds a place on the reader's table.

Our affairs are directed by a board selected from every walk in life fitted to aid in our great endeavor. The ablest business men of our city guide its financial interests. By their side sit those who have explored the frozen regions of the north and others who have labored under tropical suns. Astronomers who follow the orbits of celestial worlds, geologists who read the testimony of the rocks and tell us the story of the earth on which we dwell; physicists to measure the stress and strain of those great cosmic forces that shape our globe, and geodesists to compute its resultant form; botanists to trace the migrations of plant life and meteorologists to chart the winds that waft the seed; a physician to direct our studies of the relation of health to locality and a biologist who gives to each form of animal life its metes and bounds; a statistician who places in stately columns the figures that show economic development and achievements and a journalist lays for us a course through the world of letters. The world's greatest inventor gratifies our Athenian thirst for new things, and officers of the Army and of the Navy see to it that our facts are well marshaled and our conclusions prove invincible.

These men—busy men—gladly give their time to the great work of this Society, and, seeking no reward, find full compensation in the conviction that under their guidance the Society is living up to its avowed purpose to increase and diffuse geographic knowledge, and sister societies throughout the world gladden our ears by repeating the vesper anthem of the sixth day of creation when the Maker, in looking upon His work, said, "It is good."

THE TOASTMASTER

It might very fitly be said that the only reason that a man may have for the acquiring of more wealth than he needs for his own material wants is that he may give wisely and give well; that he may aid in the betterment of mankind, in the uplifting of civilization, in doing something to make the burdens of his fellows a little lighter, and to add more to the intellectual appreciation of those who study the great problems of the universe. There is no man in the world who has done more to help in that great work of uplifting mankind than that little giant, Andrew Carnegie. He does not expect to speak to you tonight, but I know that no matter where you place him, no matter from what altitude you drop him, he will always land upon his feet. Therefore I introduce to you now to give us a few words—and they are always words of inspiration when they come from him—Mr. Carnegie.

MR. ANDREW CARNEGIE

I have often been surprised in my short life, but never quite as much as at this moment. I promised to talk to the Associated Press in New York, now banqueting at the expense of the New York *Times*, and I had just spoken to the party there through the telephone. I met Commander Peary and he had just preceded me. He is not only a fellow Pennsylvanian, but he comes from the crest of the Alleghanies at Cresson, where I spent my summers when a young man. I had the pleasure of presenting to Commander Peary honorary membership of the Pennsylvania Society recently and did it in these words, and I was so glad that Master Shakespeare came to my relief: "Fellow Pennsylvanian, your hand in mine—'Yours is a triumph where honor travels in a path so narrow that but one goes abreast.'"

I listened to what you said about giving surplus wealth. Well, I said to the gentlemen and ladies I addressed last night at the Carnegie Institute here, as I pointed to the professors that were gathered from various stations, from the Pacific, from the Atlantic, and the work they had done—I pointed to the trustees who have one and all given years of their life to this work—"theirs is the credit, theirs the triumph. I only gave money—mere dross in itself—these men have given their lives, themselves, to the great work of obtaining knowledge and spreading it throughout the world, not for one country, but for all the world. No rivalry, all anxious to help each other in the obtainment of knowledge."

That is what makes human life sublime: I, who only give money, give the material body only. It is those workers who have infused into the dead, inert matter the soul within, and these are the men who are entitled to the credit. And so it is with all the money I give.

When I gave Doctor Billings one morning seventy-eight libraries for New York—that was the biggest wholesale order I have ever filled—I was met with congratulations the next morning when walking down the street. "What do you congratulate me for?" I asked. "Why, for giving New York seventy-eight libraries," was the answer. "Cannot receive your congratulations, gentlemen," was my reply, "but if you will congratulate me upon the bargain I made with New York, by which she agreed to maintain seventy-eight branch libraries free to all the people, shake."

I thank you for inviting me here. I thank you gentlemen for your applause and ladies for your smiles. I am the happiest man in the world, because I know that it is not what I have done that I pride myself upon. It is rather upon what I have induced others to do. Ladies and gentlemen, let me assure you I make splendid bargains with all the money that I apparently give away for nothing.

THE TOASTMASTER

Mr. Carnegie gives all the credit to those who are doing the work under his beneficence, but I would say to him that that good old Scotch brain of his never gave a dollar that he did not in his wonderful divination see far at the end some beneficent purpose, and I would say to him that a stream never rises higher, sir, than its source.

We have on our Board of Management, I am proud to say, a very wide diversity of talent, and I shall introduce now Admiral Chester, of the United States Navy, formerly Director of the Naval Observatory, who had charge of the party that went to Africa several years ago to view and to observe the eclipse, and who has done a great deal of highly creditable scientific work. We shall ask him to say a few words with regard to the work of Commander Peary in the polar regions during the past 20 years.

TWENTY YEARS' SERVICE IN THE ARCTIC—REAR ADMIRAL COLBY M. CHESTER, U. S. NAVY

My distinguished colleague has given an account of the objects of the National Geographic Society, and it is my privilege to present a brief statement of the work done by our doubly honored and highly esteemed member, Commander Peary, work that has resulted in such signal success as to probably make him the honorary member of nearly all geographic societies of the world.

Beginning back in 1886, Mr. R. E. Peary, then a young civil engineer of the U. S. Navy, originated and put into operation an entirely new project for Arctic exploration, and with a

Dane, Maigaard, reached a point near Disco, Greenland, some 50 miles from the sea. With the experience and whetted appetite for Arctic exploration gained on this trip, he soon organized a second voyage to the Polar Seas and landed at McCormick Bay, in August, 1891, and although his leg was broken in crossing Melville Bay, and he had nothing more than an Arctic winter and its attendant discomforts before him, he persisted in his determination to go north, and but few people can realize what he courageously must have passed through during that long Arctic night.

His primary object was to study the Esquimos with a view to utilizing them as a force with which to eventually reach the North Pole, and he took upon himself their habits and customs to better enable him to gain their confidence and command them when ready for the campaign quite on the same principle as our army has organized Porto Rican and Philippine Scouts to Jeal with military subjects which the natives of the country can best negotiate.

Early the following spring Peary, now able to travel, made a brilliant sledge journey of 1,300 miles, crossing the divide of 5,000 feet elevation between Whale Sound and Kane Sea, in Greenland, reaching the northern edge of the inland ice, near 82° north latitude, and discovering Independence Bay.

Again in 1894, after struggling and sacrificing his personal comfort and means to raise funds for his third expedition, we find Peary back in the frozen north with a slightly increased force, making a remarkable sledge journey of 134 miles in 13 days to an elevation of 5,500 feet.

Here he was met by violent gales and cold weather, and with his dogs dying and his men disabled, he sent his main party back to the coast, while with almost superhuman effort he plodded on another 85 miles to the good, only to be finally overcome by the elements and forced to return to his base of supplies.

In spite of the fact that he had insufficient food and fuel and that there was but little hope of replenishment, Peary would not return to the United States when the visiting steamer *Falcon* arrived in 1894 to take him back, and he spent the following winter in accumulating the resources of the region at Bowdoin Bay, living with Lee and his ever faithful Hensen as the Eskimos live, and gaining recruits for the next march to the north.

This began in April, 1895. With his two men and 63 dogs he had made but three marches when one of his Eskimos deserted with the outfit he had struggled so hard to accumulate; but Peary, undiscouraged, pushed on.

After a journey full of hardships such as had never been successfully overcome on any previous Arctic voyage, he again reached Independence Bay, whence he returned to Bowdoin Bay, with man and beast on the verge of starvation and everything but Peary's indomitable pluck entirely exhausted.

On board the little steamer *Kite* his party reached Newfoundland, September 21, 1895, and thus ended the third expedition.

General Greely speaks of this trip as follows: "If Peary's advance beyond his buried cache (on the highlands of Greenland) was one of the rashest of Arctic journeys, yet the courage, fertility of resource, and physical endurance displayed by him and his companions placed their efforts among the most notable in Arctic sledging."

Peary by this time had a thorough knowledge of the men with whom he was to finally reach the goal for which so many generations have struggled in vain. He had weeded out the dishonest ones, honored the good ones, and educated them all.

In June, 1898, Peary left New York on board the *Windward* for a four-years' expedition against the pole, this time carrying on explorations on the west shores of Baffin Bay, where he determined the continuity of Ellesmere and Grinnell Lands, and in December he was badly crippled and nearly lost his life, his feet being so badly frozen as to cause the loss of eight toes by amputation, yet he took the field again in a few weeks after the operation. In the spring he discovered Cannon Bay, and probably Heiberg Land. The winter of 1899–1900 was spent at Etah, from which place he made his first effort to reach the pole. After following the west coast of Greenland to the most northern point in about 83° 35′ north, he started north over the polar pack, but could only make good about 20 miles of ice travel before turning back in latitude 83° 54′ north. Though the North Pole was not reached, he made a valuable contribution to geography by the discovery that Greenland was an island.

In the following year, 1901, Peary again made the attempt to reach the pole by the Cape Hecla route, but was forced to abandon the attempt in April.

Still undismayed, Peary started again for the goal in February, 1902, proceeding from Payer Harbor to Fort Couger in twelve wonderful marches, and covering 400 miles in one month, with temperature ranging from −38° to −57°. Leaving the land at Cape Hecla on April 6 with seven men and six dog sledges, he now surpassed all previous explorers and attained the highest latitude reached in the Western Hemisphere, 84° 17′ north latitude.

For the sixth time Commander Peary started on his quest for the pole in July, 1905, leaving New York in the *Roosevelt*, a powerful steamer with auxiliary sailing power, the first vessel to be built in America for Arctic work, for which she was designed especially by the Commander. Fighting her way up through Kane Basin and Kennedy Channel by the Baffin Bay route, she reached Point Sheridan, on the north coast of Grant Land, where winter camp was made. Early the following spring he divided his force into four parties, each with its sledges and dogs, Eskimo drivers and hunters. This expedition is of such recent event that I need not remind you of it. Suffice it to say that now after having occupied points, "one on the most northerly point of Grant Land, and thus of the North American Archipelago; another on the most northerly point of Greenland, and the third on the northern point of Peary Land, the most northerly point in the world ever visited by man, he wins the pennant for highest north in latitude 87° 6′."

All this was a schooling for that "last great struggle to plant the American flag at the pole," the story concerning which the members of the National Geographic Society have been privileged to hear from our honored guest's own lips. Was there ever a campaign carried out after so much physical and mental effort as Peary's last? If, as Dr. Lyman Abbott has said, its Commander has done nothing else, he has taught the youth of our country the lesson of hard work and perseverance to their everlasting benefit.

Remember the last and final effort of his life in this direction was based on an original design. As he says, "the Eskimos with their dogs are the factors that make the search for the pole feasible."

He became one of the tribe—the leader of the tribe. They called him their father; he called them his children. A theme could be written on this one text, and yet how little it is understood except by those who have been Peary's companions.

Captain Bartlett told me that the Eskimos would follow the Commander as they would no other man under the sun; that they were afraid of the sea ice as a little child was of the sea water, but they would follow Peary anywhere; that there was not another living man that could get an Eskimo far away from the land; that even Peary had doubts on this subject at times, and he would say confidentially to his ever faithful assistant, Bartlett, "Are there any signs of desertions?" to which the latter would reply, with a strong voice but fearful heart, "Oh, no, don't think of it; they will follow you to the last," and so they did. I am satisfied that Bartlett was right—that while their love was tested to the extreme the Eskimos would follow Peary to the ends of the earth, but that they could be led by no other man more than "two sleeps" from land.

After returning from this last expedition I heard Peary say once, "I can never go again to the Arctic regions; I am getting too old," but his never-say-die grit overcame his yearning for the home life and rest he so much needed, and he is soon in training for the death struggle of his life. Acting under the laws of Congress, to the effect that as far as practicable all hydrographic work of the U. S. Coast and Geodetic Survey shall be done by naval officers, he was detailed by direction of President Roosevelt, the patron of all such efforts as Peary's, to that department to carry on hydrographic investigation in Ardic seas in association with the Peary Arctic Club of New York. And let me say here

that the one sounding of 1,500 fathoms without reaching bottom made by Peary near the pole is worth to the country more than all the money expended in the entire expedition, but the great mass of scientific data accumulated in his 23 years of effort has enriched the land beyond the expenditure of any possible amount of money.

The last of Peary's campaigns was a masterpiece of strategy. His force was divided into four grand divisions, led by brilliant chiefs. We can hardly overestimate the value of this organization.

I would call your attention right here to the selection of Captain Bartlett for the command of his fourth division, the post of honor. Remember that this was the one man who alone was fully competent to take the *Roosevelt* from her ice anchorage at the farthest north of any previous navigation back to civilization with all her priceless cargo of Arctic heroes. To take the second in command from this important post for a forlorn hope was beyond the borders of rashness—it was tempting Providence. Read the story of the *Polaris* expedition, and you will find that by all good rights Bartlett should never have left his ship.

But overcome by his regard for his faithful assistant, by the knowledge of Bartlett's great value to the land party, as well as by his desire to do honor to our kindred race, living under the cross of Saint George, he was given the post of honor—the advance, when it meant that had the expedition ended at latitude 87° 48' north, the second in command would become the first in honor, for he first reached this parallel two hours ahead of the main party. As it is, Bartlett hangs on his escutcheon "The Highest North" up to that time, to give away only to his chief in the still higher claim of "no north, no south, no east, no west."

Even if Peary dared do so, he could not have given the charge of his highly honored returning party to any other man under his command and do justice to those faithful children of his who were entitled to his protection. As far as a witness to Peary reaching the pole is concerned, if he needed one, he had the best one living—Hensen—a faithful colored man whose truthfulness had been tested in twenty-three years of manly and intelligent effort with his chief. Besides this, he was a man fully competent to at least record observations, and it is believed he could have made them himself.

I have often been asked what is Commander Peary's real title in the navy, and some have questioned the propriety of my calling him Commander. While Commander Peary is not a commander in the navy, he belongs to one of the most important and highly respected corps of the service—the Corps of Civil Engineers—and really outranks, or soon will do so, every commander in the navy.

However this may be, if, after being in command of the Peary Arctic expeditions for nearly twenty-three years, displaying the highest degree of executive and administrative ability, he is not a commander, then I do not know what the term implies.

The North Polar Arctic Expedition of 1908-1909, led by Commander Peary, was not a "dash to the pole," as it is popularly termed by the public, but was a grand campaign laid out on truly military lines like one of Napoleon's brilliant inspirations, and as original in conception as any of that great soldier's. Peary first went through a long span of years in the study of Arctic conditions and in the preparation of the force he was to handle. This, when ready,

was followed by an advance of his lines from the east, and resulted in the discovery of the insularity of Greenland, and that the route to the pole was not landward. He then retreated to reconnoiter and find a weak point in his adversary's defenses. After a while he tried to blaze another trail, but was driven back by the elements, those great forces of nature before which man is impotent. While his advance here was made from a base west of the position first attempted, it led him into fields where the ice was broken, and the leads—"those nightmares of Arctic explorers," as Peary calls them—left him no recourse but to retreat again.

The final assault on the North Pole, the best defended and long resisting stronghold of nature, was begun from a point still farther west, where the land jutted out into the Arctic Sea of ice much nearer the pole than any other land from which an advance was possible. From here was begun that "last of the world's great stories" which so simply and modestly, and yet so graphically, has been told by him.

The forces were led up by divisions with marvelous precision and discharged their weapons, the only ones possible to use in this campaign—provisions—and then fell back, leaving the Commander on the one hundred and thirtieth-mile line to begin the real "dash to the pole." From this point began the "Charge of the Light Brigade" that ended successfully a campaign comparable with those of Alexander, Napoleon, or Grant. Long after all of us have passed away, Peary's name will be emblazoned on the scroll of fame as one of the great commanders of the world.

THE TOASTMASTER

It is certain that in all the history of our Arctic exploration there is one commanding figure that stands out preeminent. It is fitting that now at this time I should give a brief recount of what will not be celebrated here tonight, but what is essential as we are step by step leading up to the honor of this great American.

He was born in Cresson, Pa., in 1856; was graduated from Bowdoin College in 1877; entered the United States Navy as civil engineer in 1881; was assistant engineer in the Nicaraguan Ship Canal under Government orders in 1884–85; was engineer in charge of the Nicaraguan Canal survey in 1887–88; in 1886 made a reconnaissance of the Greenland icecap; was chief of the Arctic expedition sent by the Academy of Natural Science of Philadelphia in 1891–92 to the northeast angle of Greenland; discovered and named Melville and Heilprin Land lying beyond Greenland; received the Patron's gold medal of the Royal Geographical Society of London and the medal of the Royal Geographical Society of Edinburg for determining the insularity of Greenland; made a study of the little Ardic islanders; in 1894 discovered three meteorites, one of which, the largest known to exist, weighed ninety tons; in 1896–97 brought these meteorites from Cape York to the United States. Commanded the Arctic expeditions under the auspices of the Peary Arctic Club of New York in 1898 to 1906, on which expeditions he rounded the northern extremity of Greenland Archipelago, the last of the great land groups, naming the most northerly land in the world, which is situated at 83° 39′ north latitude, and attaining the highest north at 87° 6′, for which he was awarded the Kane gold medal by the Philadelphia Geographical Society, the Daly gold medal of the American Geographical Society of New York, and the Hubbard medal of the National Geographic Society.

In 1908, under the auspices of the Peary Arctic Club of New York, in the good ship *Roosevelt*, commanded by that indomitable commander, Captain Bartlett, he again sailed for the north. No expedition ever was more perfectly planned or efficiently manned and officered. Why, it was the result of twenty years of a master mind, and the North Pole was reached on April 6, 1909. This was accomplished not only by the expenditure of tremendous physical energy, but by the employment of a high degree of intellect in planning to conserve this energy and to expend it so as to gain the greatest possible efficiency. In no other way could the North Pole ever be attained over land and over ice and water. The time may come—I believe it will come within a decade—when we shall fly over these regions that have seen so much heroic endeavor by the hardy men of nations whose representatives are gathered with us tonight, and I am of the opinion that this is the last great struggle to accomplish the pole overland.

But now, Commander Robert E. Peary, in presenting to you the special medal of the National Geographic Society, in recognition of an achievement that has brought honor to the American people, I wish to add that in all of your twenty years of heroic endeavor there has never been a time when any man associated with you, or any other person, has ever doubted your manly integrity or questioned for one moment your veracity. The American people were willing to believe that you had attained the pole by your simple statement. But science is critical. It accepts no word. It renders no decision without the proof.

And again I compliment you on the fact that before you received honors from any other source you diligently sought to present your credentials and to have them received and certified to by a competent tribunal. Those records were submitted—records made in the Arctic, not edited or prepared. I had the opportunity to meet with the committee and see the original data, and am satisfied that there was not an "i" dotted or a "t" crossed from the time the record was made, far away there in the cold fastnesses of the north. And so the decision was rendered in accordance with your claims.

And now, in presenting you with the medal of the National Geographic Society—which is voted to you by the representatives of more than fifty thousand people, thinking, active working people in the world, through its Board of Managers of twenty-four, representing nearly every type of scientific knowledge—I wish to say, sir, that in honoring you as the man we honor not only our Society, but—I speak for our guests—honor ourselves.

RESPONSE BY COMMANDER PEARY

President Moore, ladies and gentlemen of the National Geographic Society: I cannot tell you how deeply I appreciate the words of your President, how deeply I have appreciated the chivalrous, magnanimous speeches of those distinguished representatives of two great nations whose own men have done magnificent work in the Arctic regions, and who have kindly spoken here tonight; how much I have appreciated those clear, concise remarks of our greatest philanthropist; how much I have appreciated the friendly words of Admiral Chester.

Far deeper than words is my appreciation of this magnificent trophy, conveying the faith and approval of this great Geographical Society, and awarded in connection with the most extraordinary state of affairs that has ever happened in the entire history of exploration and discovery.

It is particularly appropriate that the greatest Geographical Society in the Western Hemisphere should be the first to officially recognize the winning of the last great geographical prize which the world had to offer, an accomplishment characterized by your distinguished committee as "the greatest which the Society can ever have opportunity to honor."

But mine is only a portion of the credit for which this trophy stands. Had it not been for the unswerving faith and backing (both moral and financial) of Morris K. Jesup, organizer and first President of the Peary Arctic Club; had it not been for the equally unswerving faith and backing of General Thomas H. Hubbard, the present President of the Club, and the members and friends of the Club who have furnished all the funds for the work; had it not been for the splendid loyalty, enthusiasm, energy, and endurance of the members of my party, from Captain Bartlett down, we should not have the North Pole here with us tonight.

As copartner with and representative and proxy for those whom I have mentioned, I accept your magnificent medal with feelings of the liveliest pride and gratification.

Permit me to convey to the Board of Managers of the Society, and through them to the Society itself, my own and my friends' acknowledgments for its instant perception and acceptance of the duties of its position, and its definite and courageous stand at a time when a stand for the truth meant becoming a target for the most virulent attacks from the ignorant, the vicious, and the deluded.

I wish also to convey the thanks of my friends and myself to that brother officer of superb personal and professional reputation, whose clear insight, constitutional hatred of a lie, and unanswerable arguments have done so much toward clearing the atmosphere, Admiral Chester.

Thinking men and officers accustomed to questions of personal and public duty and responsibility have understood matters from the first, and the public now appears to be grasping the fact that a navy officer does not often shirk a duty, and, when an officer of the United States Navy makes a deliberate statement concerning matters of which he has cognizance, that statement is, at all times and under all circumstances, to be taken absolutely at par.

The fundamental keynote of success in the last expedition of the Peary Arctic Club, which, on the 6th of April, 1909, discovered the North Pole, was *experience*.

If the pole could have been won by inexperience, or by a happy combination of fortuitous circumstances, it would have been won long ago.

Nor was it to be won by courage and endurance alone; if it were, England would have had the prize years ago, Norway would have had it in '95 when Nansen and Johansen cast themselves adrift into the unknown, and Italy would have attained it in 1900, when Abruzzi drove her colors to the front in spite of indescribable obstacles.

Accumulated experience, persistence, profiting by mistakes through a long series of years (the prime factors of success in any great work, whether it be the establishing of an enormous industry, the perfecting of a world-reaching invention, or the moulding of a nation)—these were the essentials which permitted the discovery of the pole by the last expedition of the Peary Arctic Club, and the essentials without which it cannot be reached again.

Let me call to your attention that the last expedition of the Peary Arctic Club had at its command the practical experience of twenty-three years of work in one field; that it had at its command a ship specially built for the work, after years of experience, tested in one voyage and then modified as the result of that test; that it had at its command a veteran personnel largely selected from the membership of a previous expedition; that it had at its command the pick and flower of the hardiest and most experienced men of an entire Eskimo tribe; that every item of its equipment was an evolution from years of experience and practical work in the same way that the last cup defender—and winner—was an evolution from preceding international yacht races, and that it had at its command the route to the pole that is recognized by all Arctic authorities as the shortest and best.

And then let me tell you that every atom of this specialized experience and equipment, every nerve of this veteran personnel, was not only utilized but *demanded* in the successful negotiation of the 413 miles of icy chaos, along the Cape Columbia route to the pole, *the route which is 100 miles shorter* EACH WAY *than any other route around the entire periphery* of the Polar Sea.

Here in this magnificent trophy of your great Society lies the final chapter of the last of the great geographical stories of the Western Hemisphere, beginning with the discovery of the new world, ending with the discovery of the North Pole.

Here is the cap and climax, the *finish*, the closing of the book on 400 years of history.

Here in this magnificent trophy of your great Society glitters the splendid frozen jewel of the north for which through centuries men of every nation have struggled and suffered and died—won at last and to be worn forever by the Stars and Stripes.

THE TOASTMASTER

The Board of Managers of the National Geographic Society have voted to Grove Karl Gilbert, a member of the National Academy of Sciences, and for many years an officer of the National Geographic Society, a Hubbard medal for his great achievements in geographic research during many years. Professor Gilbert is not here tonight, and his medal will be presented at a future time.

I shall introduce the Ambassador from Great Britain, one whom we all love so much and who has been with us before, to present to one of his own countrymen, Captain C. A. Bartlett, the medal for twice commanding the *Roosevelt*, and for being one of those heroic characters that have done so much to bring honor to our own nation and honor to that great nation of Great Britain.

THE AMBASSADOR FROM
GREAT BRITAIN—HON. JAMES BRYCE

Mr. Toastmaster, ladies and gentlemen: If it were not for the honorable duty that brings me to you tonight I should be very much ashamed to appear before you at so late an hour as this. But I am comforted and encouraged by the reflection, as I introduce myself, that this is a thing which can never occur again. There will never be another occasion in which a speaker will arise to present a medal to a man who has taken part in the discovery of the North Pole.

There is just one thought which in the midst of these festivities and congratulations weighs rather painfully upon me, ladies and gentlemen. For some centuries, as you have already been told, the discovery of the North Pole has been an object of curiosity, interest, and aspiration to all the civilized peoples of the world. They have thought about it, they have won-

dered when and how it would happen. A great German philosopher has observed that the pursuit of truth is even better than the possession of truth. Bold men were excited by the pursuit of the North Pole, and all the world was interested in following their deeds of daring. Now at last that pursuit has come to an end. The pole has been discovered. Commander Peary has found the pole. But the world has lost the pole. We have no longer this achievement to look forward to. The riddle has been solved, the curtain has been lifted, and was it fair to posterity to take away such an object of aspiration from it? I tremble to think, ladies and gentlemen, of what will happen when all the riddles of the earth have been solved and those countless generations that are to follow us have nothing that they do not know about this habitable globe of ours, a small globe, after all, too small for the restless and eager mind of man.

Now, having relieved my mind by this outburst of sadness, I come to the business which you have entrusted to my charge, and that is to present this medal to Captain Bartlett. It was a graceful and charming thought on your part, gentlemen of the National Geographic Society, that you should present this medal to Captain Bartlett, and I can assure you that it will be heartily appreciated in the good country to which Captain Bartlett belongs, and by those who, in other lands on the shores of many seas, live under the British Crown. I thank you and the National Geographic Society for it. But you have already had an acknowledgment by cable from the President of the Royal Geographical Society—one who bears an honored name, for he is the son of the great Charles Darwin—of the pleasure which it has given to that oldest of the Geographical Societies of the world.

Now, Captain Bartlett belongs to an ancient and famous line of Arctic explorers who have sailed under the flag of England. That line begins with the ever to be honored name of Henry Hudson, who perished in the great bay that he discovered. And it is illumined by many an illustrious name thereafter, among whom perhaps the most famous is Sir Edward Parry, who made his wonderful advance toward the pole, far out-stripping any who had gone before him; Sir John Franklin, Captains Ross and McClure, and McClintock, and many another of whom time would fail me to tell, dauntless spirits who bent their strength and their powers to the work of polar and Arctic exploration.

I remember seeing long, long ago, at meetings of the British Association and of the Royal Geographical Society in Britain, some of these ancient weatherbeaten veterans of polar exploration, and I know how it would rejoice them now to think that that for which they labored had at last been achieved. And if you want to know that the gallantry which animated those men and which made them bear cold and hunger and ill-health, and face all the perils of snowy wastes and floating ice in the pursuit of discovery, if you want to know that that spirit lives still with undiminished force in men of British stock, you have only to read the lately published narrative of the gallant effort to reach the South Pole made by Lieutenant Shackleton and his comrades, which brought them within 97 miles of that remote and perilous goal. This was done by the courage and hardihood of Lieutenant Shackleton.

Ladies and gentlemen, we are proud to think that the United States and Great Britain have been partners in this splendid work of Arctic exploration. The United States took up the work some forty years ago, and the names of Kane and Greely and others, above all of Commander Peary himself, show with what energy and spirit and courage and skill and perseverance you have pursued it.

But do not let us forget, in the pride which we feel in the achievements of the stock to which we both belong, what has been done by the other great nations of the world, to some of whose members reference has already been made, more particularly to the Duke of the Abruzzi, whose representative is present here tonight. Barentz must be remembered, and Weyprecht and Nordenskjöld. And there is another man whose wonderful feat of launching himself out upon the Arctic Sea and voyaging for many hundreds of miles upon ice floes is perhaps without parallel in history for its daring, and ought to be remembered in the presence of the Minister from Norway—I mean Dr. Fridthjof Nansen.

Now, ladies and gentlemen, I have the great honor of being asked to present this medal of your Society to Captain Bartlett. You, Captain Bartlett, belong to a calling which has always been able to boast of a host of hardy and adventurous seamen. You have been, on your own grim, tempestuous coast of Newfoundland, accustomed to all the perils of storm and iceberg, and it is in the line of your calling to know how to deal not only with the dangers that icebergs threaten, but with all the other terrors that the northern seas contain. You belong to a family which has signalized itself even in your land by the number of gallant seamen it has produced. I may state that there are so many Bartletts who have made distinguished and successful voyages on the North Atlantic coasts that this one who we see here tonight is familiarly known by his Christian name. He stands out from the other Bartletts as Captain Bob. He has had ten years' experience sailing with Commander Peary as the captain of his ships in his various expeditions. And I want to tell you that in those years that Captain Bartlett was sailing there never was a man lost upon those ships in those expeditions.

Captain Bartlett, I have the honor to present to you this medal. Brave men are always generous, and Commander Peary with characteristic generosity has acknowledged how much he owes to you. Your name will go down along with his in connection with the discovery of the North Pole, and you have in this medal a trophy which you can pass on to those who come after you as a memorial of the honor, the well-earned honor, which the National Geographic Society has paid to you.

Ladies and gentlemen, I rejoice to think that Great Britain and the United States are associated on this occasion. And as we congratulate you, Captain Bartlett, so I venture on behalf of my country to congratulate you, Commander Peary, and you, citizens of the United States, upon this splendid achievement—an achievement which will stand alone to the end of time.

RESPONSE BY CAPTAIN BARTLETT

Mr. President, ladies and gentlemen: I would ask you just to bear with me for about three minutes. I am afraid to trust myself in speaking, but I have a few words jotted down here that if you will not mind I will read off.

I have the medal that you have been kind enough to bestow upon me, and I thank you in my heart. To be thus decorated by so eminent a body as the National Geographic Society is an honor of which any man can justly feel proud. To say, however, that the notice which

you have taken of me affords me pleasure of the most genuine sort would be to state only a part of the truth. I am more than pleased. I am deeply moved at your distinguished consideration. My happiness in receiving this honor at your hands is increased by the fact that I never expected it. It is as unexpected as it is pleasant. It may be also that my appreciation of this medal is enhanced by the knowledge that its like can never be conferred again. It was struck off to memorialize a complete work, a work that is done, and well done. Commander Peary, with the pleasure that comes to me as I find myself in the midst of these honors, there comes the solid satisfaction of feeling that I have been of some assistance to a man of such sterling worth as Commander Peary (and I can look you straight in the eye, sir, and say that), a man whose heroic character and high aims make him quite worthy of the great fame that has come to him.

For the very great honor that you have shown me on account of my humble aid in the great work, I once again return my heartiest thanks.

THE TOASTMASTER

We have honored Commander Peary, but I am of the opinion that really the greatest honor that he has received tonight is when the captain of his ship said, "I can look you straight in the eye, sir, and say that. I mean it."

Now we shall have a word from General Thomas Hubbard, the President of the Peary Arctic Club, which has done so much for the accomplishment of the North Pole.

GENERAL THOMAS H. HUBBARD

Mr. President, ladies and gentlemen: The extension of time granted by the President to the earlier speakers does not apply to me, and if it did I would not avail myself of it, seeing that Mr. John Barrett is waiting to follow me, and I do not wish to cut off his time. But it would be ungracious on my part not to recognize the high honor paid by this Society to Commander Peary and Captain Bartlett, and it would be perhaps more ungracious to make a long speech in recognition of that honor and courtesy.

The Peary Arctic Club is a young institution. Commander Peary is a good deal older than the Peary Arctic Club. I do not mean to imply that he is older than each one of its individual members, but he is older than all of them put together in a corporate capacity. The Peary Arctic Club is eleven years old—an infant—and yet it has witnessed the departure and return of Commander Peary, first upon that long four years' absence in the north, when he came back and said he did not reach the pole; next, after the one year's absence, when he came back again and said he did not reach the pole. Either time he might have said that he reached it. There was nothing to contradict him. It would have been impossible to refute the statement. But each time he came back and said he did not do it. And now he has come back and has said that he did it, and your action, the action of this eminent Society, has approved his record.

The Peary Arctic Club has Commander Peary as its chief asset, and his honor is theirs. They have divided with him labor and danger. I know my hearers will say that in dividing labor the division has been unequal. He has done the labor and they have looked on, and I must admit that their attitude during his absence has been that of a passive trustee. During his presence his own activity has stimulated theirs. They

were kept active before he went away this last time, and they have been made more or less active since his return.

I beg to assure you that their activity has not included any conspiracies, has not included any attempt to destroy life, or blow up vessels, or steal records. How far they have shared his dangers I can only say by repeating the conversation that I had with him when he sailed out of the East River July 6, 1907.

It was a frightfully hot day and thoughts of the pole were refreshing. As I shook hands with him he said, "Take care of yourself," to which I replied, "It is an injunction I should give you. You have got to take care of yourself." Then his answer was, "Oh, no. One who knows the conditions of life in the Arctic regions is safer than he is in New York."

Now Commander Peary has made life and work in the Arctic regions comparatively safe. No one can make it safe to travel hundreds of miles over an ocean not frozen, but covered with floes likely at any time to be disrupted. But so far as the danger of starvation, the danger of loss of supplies, the dangers that have been fatal to former explorers—so far as these things are concerned, Commander Peary has made Arctic exploration safe.

Of the dangers to those who remained here I will not speak. All imagine what they are. They do not relate to Arctic exploration. They do not relate to ice, unless it is the ice trust, and they do not relate to water. In my opinion they relate chiefly to too abundant legislation. The other night I heard a statement from Professor McMillan, one of Commander Peary's companions, who said that the Eskimos were the happiest people in the world. Commander Peary says a trip up in the Arctic is safe as compared with the dangers of New York or of

Washington. I think the reason for that happiness of the Eskimo and the comparative danger of those who live in the cities throughout the United States is that the Eskimos are not governed by any laws except the laws of nature, and we suffer from a trinitarian government—the trinity of the legislative, executive, and judiciary. How can a people be safe and happy when laws are passed at the rate of twelve thousand a year, and when one State legislature in recent years made in one session three hundred and seventy-eight new crimes? How is it possible for the public to escape being made criminals?

But I am traveling outside of the subject of Arctic exploration and will come back so far as to say that those who have shared with Commander Peary the labor and the danger are entitled to some of the rewards. What are the rewards? The reward of the Peary Arctic Club is the great unparalleled achievement of Commander Peary, Captain Bartlett, and their companions, and that is sufficient to satisfy the ambition of the Peary Arctic Club and friends of the Commander. The recognition that he has received is not yet complete. His return has been met with some disappointments, but he must remember, as we all may, that such is the fate of explorers. Christopher Columbus at one time was sent a prisoner and in chains from the land he had discovered to the land that he had so much honored. Commander Peary has not been put in chains. In centuries to come his

achievement will be recognized, and in behalf of the Peary Arctic Club I thank the members of the National Geographic Society that they have not waited for the lapse of centuries before recognizing the acts and the achievement of Commander Peary.

THE TOASTMASTER

We approach the South Pole from South America, and in closing this meeting I shall ask Mr. Barrett to pronounce the benediction.

MR. JOHN BARRETT,
DIRECTOR OF THE INTERNATIONAL
BUREAU OF AMERICAN REPUBLICS

Mr. President, ladies and gentlemen: In memory of the lateness of the hour I congratulate President Moore and the officers of this Society and Commander Peary upon the significance and success of this banquet. I have only one observation to make, and that is, let us remember with reference to the future that the North Pole is not the only pole; that there is also a South Pole; that there is a great southland as well as a northland, an Antarctic as well as an Arctic Circle. And may we all gather here, possibly in a year or two years, to present a medal to that hero who shall discover the South Pole, whether he carry the flag of the United States, of Great Britain, or Italy, or France, or of that country which may produce a hero who may emulate the example of Robert E. Peary.

PEARY AS A LEADER

Incidents from the Life of the Discoverer of the North Pole Told by One of His Lieutenants on the Expedition Which Reached the Goal

By Donald B. MacMillan

"STARS AND STRIPES nailed to the Pole!"

The accomplishment of that which had been declared repeatedly to be the impossible, that which our strongest nations had striven to do for more than three hundred years, at the cost of many lives and the expenditure of millions of dollars, demanded great leadership.

What manner of man was this who persuaded the polar Eskimos to penetrate to the interior of the great *ser-mik-suah*, the abode of evil spirits; induced them to leave their homes and journey seven hundred miles due north; to travel out over the drift-ice of the Polar Sea so far that they declared that they would never again see their wives and children?

What was the secret of that power which he possessed over his white men that, had he wished, they would have followed him through broken ice, would have crossed treacherous thin leads, surmounted pressure ridges, and clung to him until the last ounce of food was gone and the last dog eaten?

We find the key to Rear Admiral Robert E. Peary's character in his reply to the late ex-President Roosevelt upon the presentation of the Hubbard Medal of the National Geographic Society upon the explorer's return in 1906 from the world's record of "Farthest North," when he said:

"The true explorer does his work not for any hopes of reward or honor, but because the thing which he has set himself to do is a part of his being and must be accomplished for the sake of its accomplishment.

"To me the final and complete solution of the polar mystery, which has engaged the best thought and interests of some of the best men of the most vigorous and enlightened nations of the world for more than three centuries, and which today stirs the heart of every man or woman whose veins hold red blood, is the thing which should be done for the honor and credit of this country, the thing which it is intended that I should do, and the thing that I must do."

Here we have energy, purpose, determination, and love of country—some of the essentials of a great leader, and as such we who had the honor of serving under him like to think of him, and such we know he was.[. . .]

NO MISUNDERSTANDING ON THE PART OF PEARY'S ASSOCIATES

What young man with red blood wouldn't follow such a man and spend every ounce of his energy to help place him at the goal of his ambition? Not one who signed his contract in the old Grand Union Hotel in New York expected to go to the Pole; not a man went north for that purpose. Each wanted to do his little and that little his best to place Peary there. Such was our admiration for this great explorer. I write this in answer to the oft-repeated statement that Peary's men were very much disappointed in not being permitted to accompany their commander to his last camp.

We entered upon this enterprise with no misunderstanding. We knew what we were facing, for we had followed him in our reading for years. We knew that this was probably his last attempt, and that he might go beyond the limit of safety, but, if so, then we all wanted to be with him and were eager for the start.

As we steamed along the Labrador coast and out into the ice of Baffin Bay, we began to know our commander and were drawn strangely toward the man whom we recognized as one thoroughly versed in ice technique—a master of his profession. We often recalled the parting words of President Roosevelt at Oyster Bay: "Peary, I believe in you, and if it is possible for man to get there, I know you'll do it!"

We all had this same faith in the man, and now that we saw him in action, that faith was even strengthened.

Decks were cleared for our battle in Melville Bay. Holds were carefully restored; necessary food and equipment made readily accessible; boats supplied with provisions, rifles, and ammunition for a retreat following a possible loss of our ship, and all without a single *order* from the man who has been called tyrant and martinet. To us, his assistants, it was always: "I would like to have you do this"; "Some time today"; "Tomorrow will do," etc. We were amazed, for we did not expect such consideration. Kindness toward his men was apparent at every stage of our voyage.

Borup was summoned to Peary's cabin from the after hold, where he was miserably seasick but pluckily sticking to his job of packing away skins, with now and then a dash to the rail. He returned an hour later, enthusiastic over his visit and over the kindness shown him by the leader of the expedition.

PEARY REVERED BY THE ESKIMOS

Those happy days of wending our way northward in and out between floes and icebergs passed all too quickly. Finally that day arrived when we passed in under the big hills of Meteorite Island and heard the glad cry of those

AN ESKIMO SEXTET
ON THE MAIN DECK OF PEARY'S ARCTIC SHIP "ROOSEVELT"

Far North natives upon beholding "Peary-ark-suah" (Big Peary) back again.

Let there be no doubt as to Peary's popularity in the Far North. Absolutely honest and square in all his dealings with these black-haired children of the Arctic, firm but ever just and kind in all his relations, he remains to them as the great "Nalegak." a leader or chief among men.

We can never forget this reception at Cape York—kayaks darting about the ship, the shouts of his former dog drivers, men who had starved with him on the Polar Sea, others on the shore standing at the water's edge ready to grasp the bow of our boat, women laughing, babies crying, and half-grown children with that look of mingled fear and animal curiosity.

How happy they were to see him back and how eagerly and how impatiently they awaited the word to pack their world's goods and transfer all to the deck of the *Roosevelt* for the long voyage northward.

And so it was at every village; the best men in the whole tribe awaited his call—a fact not without significance, in view of oft-repeated statements that Peary was unkind to his native help.

SHOO-E-GING-WA, A LITTLE ESKIMO GIRL OF ETAH,
AGE SEVEN

The Eskimo puppy-dogs are the common playthings of the Smith
Sound children.

INTO THE HEAVY ICE

Some three weeks later, with decks almost awash and black and fuzzy with dogs and Eskimos, the saucy-looking *Roosevelt* swung around Sunrise Point and into the heavy ice of Smith Sound, her destination the northern shores of Grant Land, far up at the edge of the Polar Sea.

Behind us, upon the shores of Foulke Flord, was a reserve of coal and food, to which Peary and his men could retreat if their ship was crushed. Such wise precaution was the result of his years of labor in the North and his repeated failures.

The successful negotiation of this last dangerous stretch Peary considered as the crucial link in the long chain of success. That no opportunity for advance should be lost was very evident from his almost constant vigil on the bridge, in the main rigging, or in the crow's nest.

Bartlett and Commander were a perfect team; the former young, intensely energetic, courageous: the latter experienced, cautious, of excellent judgment, constantly advising and holding his captain in check.

No braver man ever trod the quarter-deck than Bartlett. I sometimes think that Bob would rather lose his ship for the pure love of the fight southward in the drift-ice or in open boats than sail into port with his charge staunch, trim, and unscarred.

FARTHER NORTHWARD
THAN ANY OTHER SHIP EVER STEAMED

Together they drove their ship farther northward than any other ship ever steamed. Boats were ready for immediate launching; food lined the rail; emergency bags were packed.

Once in our winter quarters, Peary again displayed his qualities of leadership by removing from the ship everything absolutely needed for the attainment of the Pole and the retreat southward, if the vessel should be crushed, carried away by the ice, or burned.

In spite of the loss of the *Roosevelt*, the work would have been carried out as planned.

Even houses were built to shelter the large contingent of seventy-five men, women, and children.

MEN CONSTANTLY ON THE MOVE THROUGHOUT THE WINTER

With the Arctic night now coming on, the problem presented itself of how to preserve the health and happiness and good spirits until the time of our departure out over the ice of the Polar Sea, five months later.

At this stage of the battle many a leader has failed because he has not appreciated the full value of work, and necessarily *out-of-door* work, as shown by oft-repeated statement in books on the Arctic, such as: "No work can be done dur-ing the darkness of the Arctic winter"; "It is positively suicide to sledge during the winter," etc.

Peary laughed at such ideas. His men were away with crack of whip and laughter and enthusiasm almost as soon as our keel touched bottom at the edge of the Polar Sea, and they continued to come and go throughout the year, far into the interior of Grant Land, in quest of musk-oxen, caribou, and Arctic hare; for Peary, who never had a single case of scurvy on any of his expeditions, fully appreciated the value of fresh meat as an antiscorbutic.

Fresh vegetables, acids, and fruits are not necessary. This fact we have known for at least a half century, having acquired it from the ex-

ROUGH ICE IN THE POLAR BASIN
ABOUT ONE HUNDRED MILES DUE NORTHWEST OF AXEL HEIBERG LAND
An answer to the question why it has taken man more than three hundred years to reach farthest north.

perience of the American whaling captains when wintering on the shores of Baffin Land and Hudson Bay. Scurvy-stricken patients were always dispatched by them immediately to the igloos of the Eskimos, there to be restored to health by consuming raw frozen meat.

These excursions were not merely to keep us in good health and contentment; every move was directed toward the success of the expedition, geographically and scientifically. There were no schools between decks for the men, as in olden days; no weeks of preparation for farce or drama; no weekly or monthly periodical published; no roped promenade from berg to berg; no long hours in bed between meals.

We were either away with our dog teams among the mountains of Grant Land hunting reindeer, musk-oxen, or Arctic hare or were one hundred miles up or down the coast, living in snow houses, engaged in taking tidal observations, or at the ship working upon our equipment for the Polar dash.

If one word was written large upon the face of every man and upon the walls of every little stateroom in the steamship *Roosevelt*, it was the word *enthusiasm*, which may be translated into good leadership; for we felt our strength and our knowledge in Arctic matters increasing day by day and beheld an equipment being perfected which we knew must win.

KA-KO-TCHEE-A FEEDING MAC MILLAN'S TEAM AT ETAH, NORTH GREENLAND

On Arctic expeditions walrus are hunted for the purpose of obtaining the maximum of meat for dog food in the minimum of time.

BUILDING A SNOW HOUSE AT PETERAVIK,
THE SPRING HUNTING GROUND OF THE SMITH SOUND NATIVE

These are built larger than usual and with considerable care and lined with the summer tupic, for the Eskimos plan to remain here at least a month. The house is shown before the snow entrance has been added.

Certain items were so far superior to anything yet devised for Arctic work that their value, even to a novice, was obvious. Such were perfected by Peary following years of repeated struggle.

PEARY DEVISED
A NEW ARCTIC STOVE

Do not forget the great word *experience*. As an illustration, previous to the 1908 trip the most satisfactory stove for Arctic sledge-work was the so-called Primus, which converts cracked ice at 60 below zero into a gallon of tea in about 20 minutes. Peary reasoned that the more rapid his stove, the more sleep for his men at the end of the long march. He thereupon devised a stove which is so economical in fuel consumption and so quick in its action that many are almost inclined to doubt the fact that we had our gallon of tea in *nine* minutes from the time that the match was applied.

Our clothing, that of the Smith Sound Eskimo, could not be improved upon. Our food was amply sufficient for the maintenance of health and strength. Our sledges were modeled by Peary for the rough ice of the Polar Sea and skillfully fashioned by our master mechanic, Matt Henson. Our equipment was without a doubt the most nearly perfect yet devised for Polar work.

Peary's plan for advance and attack upon the Pole, based upon his experience and failure in 1906, was unique and a large factor in his final success.

From the time when one leaves the northern shores of Grant Land or Greenland, one must depend wholly upon the food on the sledges for sustenance of men and dogs. An occasional bear or seal might be secured, but such would be the exception, as proved by the experience of Nansen, Sverdrup, Captain Cagni, Peary, and every man who has been north of 84°.

To feed Peary and his men until he was within striking distance of the Pole and self-supporting for the five hundred miles of the return trip was the work assigned to the so-called supporting parties under the command of Henson, Bartlett, Marvin, Borup, Goodsell, and myself.

Every five days a white man and his Eskimos were to return to land with an amount of food equal to one-half consumed in the outward trip, with orders to double march, and if held up by open water to eat the dogs. The work of this division was done; it was no longer needed in a task where one's life might depend upon ounces, not pounds; where every additional particle of food is a synonym for miles of travel, and where the last ounce might mean the last mile and success in one's life-work.

AN INSTANCE OF HEROIC SACRIFICE

In general, the American people have minimized the dangers of travel on the Polar Sea and have overestimated the narrow margin of safety of even a small party five hundred miles from land.

The presence of one man not absolutely needed in the work endangers the lives of all,

for that man must be fed and must receive an equal amount of the last bite.

Do you remember the brave Oates, of the Scott starvation party, who, realizing that his presence meant the loss of all, calmly remarked to his commander, "I am going out for a little while; I may not come back"?

With the dropping of the tent flap and the disappearing of that stumbling frost-bitten form into the swirling snows of the Antarctic ice-cap, there ended the most pathetic and the most heart-stirring scene ever enacted upon the stage of Polar work. All honor to such a hero!

Every white man realized what the success of this trip meant to Peary, and each man knew that the sooner he returned to land after he had finished his work, the better the chances of Peary reaching his goal.

When we heard the words, "You are to go back tomorrow," let me emphasize the fact that every man did so cheerfully and willingly, knowing that it was for the best interests of the expedition. No man expected to go at the start and no man complained at the finish.

Peary owed it to himself, to his friends, to his country, to rid himself of all encumbrances, of all superfluous material, and strip for action. It was his fight now, not ours; ours only just as long as we were needed.

And the negro? He was indispensable to Peary and of more real value than the combined services of all four white men. With years of experience equal to that of Peary himself, an expert dog-driver, a master mechanic, physically strong, most popular with the Eskimos, talking the language like a native, clean full of grit, he went to the Pole with Peary because he was easily the most efficient of all Peary's assistants.

THE ONLY MAN
BESIDES ADMIRAL PEARY AND FOUR ESKIMOS
WHO STOOD AT THE TOP OF THE WORLD

Matthew Henson, the expert assistant, had been with Peary since his second expedition to Nicaragua, in 1887, and on all his Arctic expeditions except the first, in 1886. The leader considered him the best dog-driver living, except some of the best of the Eskimo hunters themselves.

UNREASONABLE DOUBT CAUSED BY PEARY'S SPEED

Weeks later the little band of six returned, clearly revealing the terrible strain and anxiety during that rapid dash to land over ice fields which threatened to be rent asunder by the high tides of the approaching full moon. In fact, the work was *too* well done, as many a doubt as to Peary's achievement was based upon the time of his return.

During the days of that most unfortunate controversy enough consideration was not given by the public to the following all-important facts:

First. Peary's supporting parties placed him at nearly the 88th parallel.

Second. The observations at this point were taken and signed by Captain Bartlett, of the *Roosevelt*.

Third. From this point on Peary had five well-provisioned sledges. five of the best men of 25, 48 of the best dogs of 250, and only 120 miles to go.

Fourth. The trail to land was well marked and broken ends knit together by the retreat of the various divisions.

A MEMBER OF THE MAC MILLAN EXPEDITION FINDING PEARY'S CABIN
AND RECORD AT THE NORTHERN END OF AXEL HEIBERG LAND, MAY, 1914

The Arctic explorer reached this point in June, 1906, on his return from "Farthest North," 87° 6′, reached in April of that year.

Fifth. All expeditions for a half century have double-marched and even triple-marched on the return trip.

How often have I heard the assertion that Peary told none of his men that he had reached the Pole until he learned of Dr. Cook's attainment! Far up on the northern shores of Grant Land, at the edge of the Polar Sea, there stands a cairn, Peary's announcement of the attainment of his life's work, built there *twelve weeks* before we reached civilization. He did not forget his men. The names not only of his assistants, but of every man on board the *Roosevelt*, are written there and placed under glass as a protection against the weather.

PEARY DELAYS NEWS OF HIS TRIUMPH IN ORDER TO HELP ESKIMOS

Upon our arrival at Etah, several weeks later, Dr. Cook's two Eskimo dog drivers, E-took-a-shoo and Ah-pellah, came on board and told us that in company with Cook they had been living down in Jones Sound for nearly a year, and that at no time had they been farther north than a spot which they indicated on the map close to the northern shores of Axel Heiberg Land, distant 500 miles from the Pole.

Naturally eager to steam southward to proclaim to the world the news of his discovery after so many years of hardship, yet Peary felt that his first duty was toward his Eskimos, those natives who made it possible for him to win out. And there we remained, killing walrus and supplying them with food for the long winter night to come, while Cook was wearing roses and being feted by kings and queens.

Peary's attitude upon reaching the Labrador coast has been grossly misunderstood. Not only did he not mention his rival's name in his first telegrams, but expressly requested us to refrain from doing so; and this in view of the fact that he knew that an impostor was being proclaimed as the real discoverer. He was not, however, to be permitted to retain this rôle of stoic.

We steamed southward from Indian Harbor, and upon our arrival at Battle Harbor our Commander was met by a flood of telegrams from the press and from various geographical and scientific societies at home and abroad, all requesting that he give them his honest opinion as to Dr. Cook's achievement.

What should he do?

At this crucial point in his career the average man believes that Peary failed. But the average man has not slept with his back against a sledge at fifty and sixty degrees below zero, with biting winds whipping the snow over his body, dead tired with the day's work; has not crossed treacherous black ice on snow-shoes; has not staggered back beaten to his little hut, followed by one shadow—of a dog; has not returned to home, family, and friends year after year with the one word failure on his lips; has not in the flush of victory seen an impostor bowing to the plaudits of the multitude.

Was his one public telegram in answer to urgent requests too severe in condemnation of one whose claims have since been discredited by every scientific society in the world: "Dr. Cook has handed the people a gold brick. When he claims to have discovered the Pole over his own signature, I shall have something decidedly interesting to say"?

Peary could have shifted the responsibility for that answer upon Captain Bartlett or any of his assistants; but all who know Peary know that the thought of doing so never entered his mind, as he restlessly paced the floor of his little cabin in that northern port.

That bitter controversy is dismissed today with "most unfortunate"!

As we steamed southward on our last lap with this great explorer, we often reviewed the year that had gone so quickly, and our relations with our leader, all so pleasant.

Ever kind and thoughtful and considerate of his young and inexperienced men, he treated them as a father would treat his sons. He helped us lash and pack our sledges, untangled and repaired our frozen and knotted traces.

When struggling along far in the rear, with refractory dogs and heavy loads, an Eskimo would often be detailed to relieve us of a part of our load and pilot us safely across an open lead, and if we arrived with frost-bitten face, it was often the Commander's warm hand that brought the blood back to the surface.

SOLICITUDE FOR HIS ASSOCIATES' WELFARE ONE OF PEARY'S NOTEWORTHY TRAITS

I well remember falling through the ice at 59 below zero. With sealskin boots filled with water and rapidly stiffening clothes, I arrived at our encampment of snow houses. He beat the ice from my bearskin pants, pulled off my boots, and wiped my feet and legs with the inside of his warm shirt. And when covered with blood, a heavy 40-82 bullet having passed through my arm, into my shoulder, and out through the back, and clipping the side of one finger, he re-marked: "I would much rather had that thing happen to me than to you!"

This does not sound like "martinet" or "tyrant" or "unkind to his men." His last

words to Marvin, lost on the return, "Be care-ful of the leads, my boy," is characteristic of the man.

Is it any wonder, then, that we as assis-tants, when we heard the blowing of the whistles of Sydney, N. S.; beheld the line of craft cir-cling out to escort us into the harbor; saw wav-ing flags and docks black with people, should be almost sorry that he had won out?

We knew that never again would we have the honor and the pleasure of serving under such a leader.

PEARY'S HUT AT CAPE SABINE,
FROM WHICH THE EXPLORER MADE HIS DASH TOWARD THE POLE IN 1900

This refuge was formerly the deck-house of the steamship *Windward*, used by Peary in his 1898–1902 Expe-dition.

PEARY'S EXPLORATIONS
IN THE FAR NORTH

By Gilbert Grosvenor

President of the National Geographic Society

THE struggle for the North Pole began nearly one hundred years before the landing of the Pilgrim Fathers at Plymouth Rock, being inaugurated (1527) by that king of many distinctions, Henry VIII of England.

Scores of hardy navigators—British, French, Dutch, German, Scandinavian, and Russian—followed Davis, all seeking to hew across the Pole the much-coveted short route to China and the Indies. The rivalry was keen and costly in lives, ships, and treasures; but from the time of Henry VIII for three and one-half centuries, or until 1882 (with the exception of 1594-1606, when, through William Barents, the Dutch held the record), Great Britain's flag was always waving nearest the top of the globe.*

*In 1882 Lockwood and Brainard, of Greely's expedition, won the record of Farthest North for the United States, and we held it until Nansen's feat of 1896.

Immense treasures of money and lives were expended by the nations to explore the northern ice world and to attain the apex of the earth; but all efforts to reach the Pole had failed, notwithstanding the unlimited sacrifice of gold and energy and blood which had been poured out without stint for nearly four centuries.

PEARY'S INTEREST IN THE ARCTIC AWAKENED IN 1886

A brief summer excursion to Greenland in 1886 aroused Robert E. Peary, a civil engineer in the United States Navy, to an interest in the Polar problem. Peary a few years previously had been graduated from Bowdoin College second in his class—a position which means unusual mental vigor in an institution which is noted for the fine scholarship and intellect of its alumni. He realized at once that the goal which had eluded so many hundreds of ambitious and dauntless men could be won only by a new method of attack.

The first Arctic problem with which Peary grappled was considered at that time in importance second only to the conquest of the Pole, namely, to determine the insularity of Greenland and the extent of its projection northward. At the very beginning of his first expedition to Greenland, in 1891, he suffered an accident which sorely taxed his patience as well as his body, and which is mentioned here as it illustrates the grit and stamina of his moral and physical make-up.

As his ship, the *Kite*, was working its way through the ice fields off the Greenland shore, a cake of ice became wedged in the rudder, causing the wheel to reverse. One of the spokes jammed Peary's leg against the casement, making it impossible to extricate himself until both bones of the leg were broken.

The party urged him to return to the United States for the winter and to resume his exploration the following year; but Peary insisted on being landed, as originally planned, at McCormick Bay, stating that the money of his friends had been invested in the project, and that he must "make good" to them.

The assiduous nursing of Mrs. Peary, aided by the bracing air, so speedily restored his strength that at the ensuing Christmas festivities which were arranged for the Eskimos he outraced on snowshoes all the natives and his own men!

HE ASCENDS THE GREENLAND ICE-CAP

In the following May, with one companion, Astrup, he ascended to the summit of the great ice-cap which covers the interior of Greenland, 5,000 to 8,000 feet in elevation, and pushed northward for 500 miles over a region where the foot of man had never trod before, in temperatures ranging from 10 degrees to 50 degrees below zero. Imagine his surprise on descending from the table-land to enter a little valley radiant with gorgeous flowers and alive with murmuring bees, where musk-oxen were lazily browsing.

This sledding journey, which he duplicated by another equally remarkable crossing of the ice-cap, three years later, defined the northern extension of Greenland and conclusively proved that it is an island instead of a continent extending to the Pole. In boldness of conception and brilliancy of results, these two crossings of Greenland are unsurpassed in Arctic history. The magnitude of Peary's feat is better appreciated when it is recalled that Nansen's historic crossing of the island was below the Arctic Circle, 1,000 miles south of Peary's latitude, where Greenland is some 250 miles wide.

HE TURNS HIS ATTENTION TO THE POLE

Peary now turned his attention to the Pole, which lay 396 geographical miles farther north than any man had penetrated on the Western Hemisphere. To get there by the American route he must break a virgin trail every mile north from Greely's 83° 24′. No one had pioneered so great a distance northward. Markham and others had attained enduring fame by advancing the flag considerably less than 100 miles, Parry had pioneered 150 miles, and Nansen 128 from his ship.

His experiences in Greenland had convinced Peary, if possible more firmly than before, that the only way of surmounting this last and most formidable barrier was to adopt the manner of life, the food, the snow houses, and the clothing of the Eskimos, who by centuries of experience had learned the most effective method of combating the rigors of Arctic weather; to utilize the game of the Northland, the Arctic reindeer, musk-ox, etc., which his explorations had proved comparatively abundant, thus with fresh meat keeping his men fit and good-tempered through the depressing winter night; and, lastly, to train the Eskimo to become his sledging crew.

In his first North Polar expedition, which lasted for four years, 1898–1902, Peary failed to get nearer than 343 miles to the Pole. Each successive year dense packs of ice blocked the passage to the Polar Ocean, compelling him to make his base approximately 700 miles from the Pole, or 200 miles south of the headquarters of Nares, too great a distance from the goal to be overcome in one short season. During this trying period, by sledging feats which in distance and physical obstacles overcome exceeded the extraordinary records made in Greenland, he explored and mapped thousands of miles of coast line of Greenland and of the islands west and north of Greenland.

PEARY LED HUNDREDS
INTO THE ARCTIC WITH ONLY
TWO TRAGIC ACCIDENTS

On the next attempt Peary insured reaching the Polar Ocean by designing and constructing the *Roosevelt*, whose resistless frame crushed its way to the desired haven on the shores of the Polar sea. From here he made that wonderful march of 1906 to 87° 6', a new world's record. Winds of unusual fury, by opening big leads, robbed him of the Pole and nearly of his life.

The last Peary expedition, 1908–1909, resulted in the discovery of the Pole and of the deep ocean surrounding it. The 396 miles from Greely's farthest had been vanquished as follows: 1900, 30 miles; 1902, 23 miles; 1906, 169 miles; 1909, 174 miles.

No better proof of the minute care with which every campaign was prearranged can be given than the fact that, though Peary has taken hundreds of men north with him on his various expeditions, he has brought them all back, and in good health, with the exception of two, who lost their lives in accidents for which the leader was in no wise responsible. What a contrast this record is to the long list of fatalities from disease, frost, shipwreck, and starvation which in the popular mind has made the word arctic synonymous with tragedy and death.

THE PRIZE OF FOUR CENTURIES
IS HIS REWARD

Thus Robert E. Peary crowned a life devoted to the exploration of the icy North and to the advancement of science by the hard-won discovery of the North Pole. The prize of four centuries of striving yielded at last to the most persistent and scientific attack ever waged against it. Peary's success was made possible by long experience, which gave him a thorough knowledge of the difficulties to be overcome, and by an unusual combination of mental and physical power—a resourcefulness which enabled him to find a way to surmount all obstacles, a tenacity and courage which knew no defeat, and a physical endowment such as Nature gives to few men.

It has been well said that the glory of Peary's achievement belongs to the world and is shared by all mankind. But we, his fellow-countrymen, who have known how he struggled those many years against discouragement and scoffing and how he persevered under financial burdens that would have crushed less stalwart shoulders, especially rejoice that he "made good at last," and that an American has become the peer of Hudson, Magellan, and Columbus.*

PEARY'S ASSOCIATION WITH THE NATIONAL GEOGRAPHIC SOCIETY

Peary's first address to the National Geographic Society was in the fall of 1888, when The Society was only a few months old. He then described an expedition which he had led across Nicaragua. He was actively associated with its work ever since those early days, and on his return from each of his expeditions to the Far North, his first public address was to the National Geographic Society. His last public appearance was on the platform of the National

* The preceding paragraphs are exracted from a brief history of North Polar explorations written by Gilbert Grosvenor for the Foreword of Admiral Peary's book, "The North Pole" (F. A. Stokes Company).

Geographic Society when in January, 1919, he introduced Stefansson, who had just returned from the Canadian North.

It was at a National Geographic Society meeting in 1907 that he was presented the Hubbard Gold Medal of The Society by President Roosevelt, and in 1909 a Special Gold Medal for his discovery of the North Pole, and later he became a member of its Board of Managers.

It was my privilege to know Admiral Peary intimately for twenty years, and I find it difficult to express my admiration and affection for his personal qualities, the bigness of his heart and personality, his loyal devotion to his friends, his generous enthusiasm at real accomplishment by others in any field, his rugged integrity, and his love for everything American.

As long as the National Geographic Society lives, its members can take pride in the fact that the organization did its utmost to help Peary "nail the Stars and Stripes to the Pole."

FURTHER READING

John Edward Weems, *Peary: The Explorer and the Man* (1967) is a major biography which is based on Peary's personal papers. See also John Edward Weems, *Race for the Pole* (1960) and Bradley Robinson *Dark Companion* (1947). The latter is an excellent account of Matthew Henson's role in Peary's expeditions. Peary's own volumes are superb adventure stories: *Northward Over the Great Ice* (1898); *Nearest the Pole* (1907); *The North Pole* (1910) and *Secrets of Polar Travel* (1917). Peary's daughter published a biography of her father, Marie P. Stafford, *Discoverer of the North Pole* (1959). *The Atlas of the North American Exploration: From the Norse Voyages to the Race to the Pole* (1998) by William H. Goetzmann and Glyndwr Williams, chronologically documents the exploration and discovery of the North Pole.

INDEX

CONTRIBUTORS

General Editor FRED L. ISRAEL is an award-winning historian. He received the Scribe's Award from the American Bar Association for his work on the Chelsea House series *The Justices of the United States Supreme Court*. A specialist in American history, he was general editor for Chelsea's *1897 Sears Roebuck Catalog*. Dr. Israel has also worked in association with Arthur M. Schlesinger, jr. on many projects, including *The History of the U.S. Presidential Elections* and *The History of U.S. Political Parties*. He is senior consulting editor on the Chelsea House series *Looking into the Past: People, Places, and Customs*, which examines past traditions, customs, and cultures of various nations.

Senior Consulting Editor ARTHUR M. SCHLESINGER, JR. is the pre-eminent American historian of our time. He won the Pulitzer Prize for his book *The Age of Jackson* (1945), and again for *A Thousand Days* (1965). This chronicle of the Kennedy Administration also won a National Book Award. He has written many other books, including a multi-volume series, *The Age of Roosevelt*. Professor Schlesinger is the Albert Schweitzer Professor of the Humanities at the City University of New York, and has been involved in several other Chelsea House projects, including the *American Statesmen* series of biographies on the most prominent figures of early American history.